men and pandas

Uniform with this volume:

MEN AND SNAKES
MEN AND APES

men

RAMONA & DESMOND MORRIS

and pandas

McGraw-Hill Book Company

New York   Toronto   London   Sydney

Library of Congress Catalog Card Number: 66–28078
43175

Printed in Great Britain
by Balding + Mansell Ltd, London and Wisbech and bound by
William Brendon & Son Ltd, Tiptree, Essex

contents

Acknowledgements   VI
Introduction   VII

The Beautiful Red Panda   9
The Giant Panda Discovered   21
The Panda Killers   45
The Panda Pursued   61
Pandas in America   79
The London Pandas   99
Post-war Pandas   115
The Panda as an Animal   145
The Appeal of the Panda   193

APPENDIX I: A Concise History of Pandas   205
APPENDIX II: Live Pandas outside the Orient—Longevity
                    Chart   211
APPENDIX III: Bamboos Acceptable to the Giant Panda   212
Bibliography   213
Index   221

acknowledgements

THE AUTHORS are grateful to the many people who have assisted in the preparation of this book. To the Zoological Society of London for providing access to their files and documents; to Granada TV for supplying valuable photographic material on Chi-Chi; to the World Wildlife Fund for useful conservation documents; to the Peking Zoo for photographs of Ming-Ming and Lin-Lin; to the British Museum for checking ancient records; and to the Librarians of the London Zoo for their repeated helpfulness. In particular we would like to thank Tony Dale, P.R.O. at the London Zoo, for valuable discussions; Professor D. B. Fry of London University for his help in preparing sound spectrograms of giant panda calls; Oliver Graham-Jones for details of Chi-Chi's hospital treatment; Dr. L. Harrison-Matthews for reading parts of the manuscript and for lending us a packet of Chinese cigarettes; Mrs. Mary Haynes and Miss Caroline Jarvis for providing us with much needed information from China; Dr. Rainer Lorenz for ascertaining details of Happy's tour of Germany in 1939; The Hon. Ivor Montagu for indispensable information and photographs from Peking; Head Keeper Sam Morton for permission to publish details from his giant panda record-book; George B. Rabb of Chicago Zoo for access to unique panda documents from the 1930s; Richard J. Reynolds for lengthy and painstaking correspondence on many aspects of recent panda history; W. G. Vanderson for devoting much time and patience to obtain special panda photographs for us; and to Dr. Geoffrey Vevers for casting his mind back over a quarter of a century with great precision, and also for lending us valuable and otherwise unobtainable books. Finally, we would like to express our gratitude to Graham Nicol and Elizabeth Stockwell of Hutchinson's for their continual encouragement and assistance throughout the production of this volume.

introduction

AT FIRST SIGHT the giant panda is an enigma. Discovered less than a century ago, it is as much loved as it is little known. It has never been seriously studied in the wild and no more than seventeen live specimens have been seen outside China. Thirty years ago the western world had encountered nothing more than stuffed specimens in a few museums. Then, in a series of dramatic moves, the giant pandas arrived. They came to America and Europe. The public saw them and were conquered. The chubby, clumsy, black-and-white form quickly became a national and then an international image. Still largely a mystery beast, this fascinating animal swiftly rose to the top of the animal popularity charts, and there it has remained ever since.

What exactly do we know about this strange creature ? What is the secret of its success ? This is the challenge we set ourselves when we started work on *Men and Pandas*. In our previous volumes in this series—*Men and Snakes* and *Men and Apes*—the problem was a different one. In both cases a great deal was already known about the animals concerned, and many volumes, both learned and popular, had already been written about them. The primary task there was one of selection and co-ordination of information from the great mass of facts available. With pandas, the problem was, by contrast, to seek out every tiny scrap of evidence from the scanty supply that existed, tucked away for the most part in obscure journals and yellowing press cuttings. The search has proved to be an exciting one, providing us with a story with some unexpected twists and several unsolved mysteries. We hope you will enjoy reading it as much as we have enjoyed our detective work in assembling it.

RM DM
Regent's Park, London

the beautiful
red panda

the beautiful red panda

CHAPTER ONE

The original portrayal of the red panda. (From *Cuvier* 1825)

IN JUNE 1825, Frédéric, son of the famous French zoologist Georges Cuvier dated, with a flourish no doubt, the first published account of an animal new to science. The popular name for this exciting discovery from the Himalayan Mountains was "the panda". In scientific circles it was known as *Ailurus fulgens*, a "fire-coloured cat" or "shining cat". Later generations thought that the choice of this particular name was unfortunate and misleading, but to Frédéric Cuvier it seemed appropriate enough. He wrote, "I propose for the generic name of this panda that of *Ailurus*, on account of its exterior resemblance to the cat and for its specific name that of *Fulgens*, because of its brilliant colours." He added that in his opinion this rare creature was quite the most handsome mammal in existence.

We see from the coloured plate accompanying Cuvier's description that the panda was an attractive medium-sized, basically rust-red animal with a bushy tail and a rather foxy white face, quite different in general appearance from the animal popularly known as the panda today. At the present time, the small red panda is usually called the lesser panda to distinguish it from its more spectacular relative the black-and-white giant panda. But, for half a century, Cuvier's *Ailurus fulgens* was the *only* panda known in the West and proved itself to be a highly interesting and unusual animal in its own right.

For many years the lesser panda remained an enigma and not a single living specimen reached European shores. When preparing his description of the animal Cuvier was obliged to work from a few remains and a general outline of its shape provided by his son-in-law, Alfred Du Vaucel. Even so, with only a skin, paws and incomplete jaw bones and teeth at his disposal, the French zoologist realized that the panda was unique, there being no evidence of any other mammal of the same type among the relics stowed away in the Paris Natural History Museum.

Despite Cuvier's efforts it is usually recognized that the real discoverer of the lesser panda was however an Englishman in Indian Service, Major-General Thomas Hardwicke, who explored the country where he was stationed in the early decades of the nineteenth century with a keen eye for animal rarities. On 6th November 1821, he read a paper before the Linnean Society of London entitled, "Description of a New Genus of the Class Mammalia, from the Himalaya Chain of Hills between Nepaul and the Snowy Mountains." The creature in question was none other than the red panda for he gave considerable detail about the external appearance of the animal and pointed out that it must rank as a new genus owing to its striking and prominent peculiarities. Of its habits the general wrote: "Its haunts are about rivers and mountain-torrents. It lives much in trees, and feeds on birds and the smaller quadrupeds. It is frequently discovered by its loud cry or call, resembling the word Wha, often repeating the same: hence is derived one of the local names by which it is known. It is also called Chitwa." Six years passed before Hardwicke's paper finally appeared in print in 1827 and so he not only lost publication priority to Frédéric Cuvier but also the honour of naming the animal.

As far as the official printed word was concerned British zoology had been indisputedly pipped at the post by its enterprising French counterpart, but it is possible that neither country should take the credit for the actual discovery of the red panda. In 1820, a Danish botanist, Nathaniel Wallich, was appointed director of the East India Company's Botanical Gardens at Calcutta. Naturally plants were his primary interest and he made a number of collecting trips to the northern mountain regions of Nepal in this connection. At the same time he also brought back animals from this particular region for both General Hardwicke and Cuvier's son-in-law, Alfred Du Vaucel, and it so happens that the area that he visited is the heart of lesser panda territory. The facts are unrecorded but this coincidence leaves us with the interesting speculation that the obliging Dane may have provided either the Englishman or the Frenchman, or both, with their red pandas.

Some twenty years passed before another European naturalist contributed to western zoology's knowledge of the Himalayan "fiery fox", or "raccoon", as the panda was popularly called. He was Brian Houghton Hodgson, who in 1845, after a stormy career in the Indian Civil Service, retired to a modest bungalow situated in a remote beauty spot in the high mountains of Sikkim. Here, for thirteen years, he led the life of a hermit and acquired the nick-name "the Darjiling recluse". Cut off from the world though he was, he none the less took the opportunity to indulge in one of his primary interests, natural history. In 1847 all his frustration and pent-up emotion about the appalling way in which Britain had neglected the study of Indian animals was unleashed in the *Journal of the Asiatic Society of Bengal*, reaching a pitch of outraged patriotism on the subject of the lesser panda.

Brian Houghton Hodgson

Cuvier, insisted the English eccentric, knew little about *Ailurus*. Even the popular name "panda" bequeathed to it by the Frenchman was outlandish. In Hodgson's view, it was scandalous that in the mid-nineteenth century the French still held a monopoly in contemporary knowledge of the Wah, as he preferred to call the red panda. He declared that Cuvier "defined or rather indicated the Genera late in his career from imperfect specimens transmitted immediately after their arrival in the East by Vaucel and Diard, gentlemen whom the Jardin des Plantes sent out to glean the harvest which English perverseness could not or would not take any sensible or intelligible steps to glean . . . I myself assisted Du Vaucel's researches with alacrity. But at the same time I stated to the leaders of this science in England what a pity it was that want of ordinary measures on their part to secure the co-operation of their countrymen in the East should thus continue to prevent England's reaping the zoological harvest of her own domains; and I pointed to my own drawings, specimens and description of the structure and habits of *Ailurus* lying unused in their hands whilst their Journal (the *Zoological Journal*) was putting forth the mere crumbs gathered from Cuvier's table . . . and whilst his active son-in-law was then preparing under my very eye and with my own aid to complete the supercession of what ought to have been from the first, and might even yet be in part, English researches. How and why my appeal failed I know not. They order these things better in France. . ."

Behind Hodgson's outburst lay a very specific and personal complaint. As we have seen, he refers to his own important information about the lesser panda being neglected and completely overlooked by the Zoological Society of London. In 1833, when he was acting as Resident in Nepal, as a Corresponding Member of the newly formed society, Hodgson had sent it "a full and careful description of the habits and of the hard and soft anatomy of *Ailurus*". This, presumably, he felt should have superseded Cuvier's description, for he was apparently unaware of General Hardwicke's paper of 1827. But, he continues, "What became of that paper I know not, and have now to regret that the original M.S. was lost with many others of great value at the period of my hurried departure for Europe." The result was that nothing of any great significance appeared on the subject of the red panda between 1825 and 1847. Hodgson therefore decided to publish what remained of his notes compiled some fifteen years previously.

Whatever its shortcomings, his article represented the sum total of information available on the lesser panda for more than two

AILURUS. *ochraceus.*

Hodgson's sketches of sleeping pandas

decades. Indeed, since no one has really studied the habits of the animal in the wild to this day and virtually nothing is known of its behaviour, except from captive specimens, he still remains an authority on the subject.

Solitary, self-taught and embittered naturalist that he was, Hodgson was none the less a keen observer of animal life. Most of his information about the red panda was obviously based on the behaviour of several live specimens which he had kept in Nepal. His sketches of the animal's sleeping postures have the realistic quality of drawings from life. Many pandas were brought to him for they were easily caught with "little speed, cunning or ferocity to protect them". Since their flesh was never eaten and their only economic value lay in the manufacture of fur caps, this lack of self-defence against man the predator was, apparently, no serious handicap. Hodgson was obviously very fond of his pandas for he wrote: "The amenity of their ordinary disposition is finely portrayed in their gentle countenances, and, as they are free from all offensive odour, they would make nice pets for ladies, particularly when young. They drink by lapping with the tongue and moderately. They hiss and spit like cats when angered, and, if extremely so, utter a short deep grunt like that of a young Bear; but ordinarily they are quite silent."

As to the panda's habits in the wild, Hodgson wrote: "They are alivorous climbers, frequenting trees much, but breeding and feeding chiefly on the ground, and having their retreat in the natural resiliences of rocks." The adults he believed are monogamous, living in pairs or small families until the next brood is about to appear at which point the mother drives the grown young away. Two offspring at a time is normal and they are born in spring or early summer. The animal sleeps a good deal during the day and has a strong aversion to bright light, but is not nocturnal in its feeding habits. It eats tuberous roots, acorns, beech mast, eggs and bamboo sprouts. "In general the wahs eschew flesh, fish, insects, reptiles, absolutely. But they love milk and ghee, and constantly make their way furtively into remote dairies and cowherd's cottages to possess themselves of these luxuries."

For many years Europe eagerly awaited the arrival of the first living panda, the animal that Cuvier had hailed as the most beautiful creature known to man. Under the circumstances it was with considerable satisfaction that the Secretary of the Zoological Society of London announced at a meeting of the Fellows on 13th May 1869, that he had received a letter from Dr J. Anderson of the Indian Museum, Calcutta. It contained the news that the three lesser pandas to be presented to the zoo by Dr. H. Simpson had

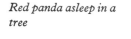

Red panda asleep in a tree

Folio sheet of panda sketches presented to the Zoological Society of London by Hodgson

The red panda from the Hodgson folio

already arrived in Calcutta, although whether they would reach English shores alive seemed doubtful. Anderson wrote: "I have taken them under my charge, and am doing all I can to mitigate their sufferings from the heat, which has been very great during the last few days, reaching as high as 95° on the cool shaded side of the house. I have a man attending to them all day; and when the sun goes down I have them carried out into a cool breezy spot. I have had a new and comfortable airy cage constructed, as the one they were in was filthy in the extreme. The original specimen, which I found at Darjeeling, and which now belongs to Dr. Simpson, is in capital condition, and may live through the heat of the Red Sea; but I doubt much if the others will."

Two of the red pandas did, in fact, die on the voyage and the third reached the London Zoo on 22nd May clinging to life by a thread. The pitiful creature was taken under the wing of the Zoo's superintendent, Abraham Dee Bartlett, or "Papa" Bartlett as he was affectionately known to the Press. At the time, the British were becoming animal conscious and Bartlett was one of the first great animal popularizers, providing the public with entertaining and instructive stories about his charges. He was a splendid figure of a man, invariably dressed in a top hat and long frock coat whether wielding a scalpel or a stable broom.

The wretched object that arrived at the Zoo was anything but lovely. This is how Bartlett described the panda: "I found the animal in a very exhausted condition, not able to stand, and so weak that it could with difficulty crawl from one end of its long cage to the other. It was suffering from frequent discharges of frothy, slimy faecal matter. This filth had so completely covered and matted its fur, that its appearance and smell were most offensive."

The official portrait of the first red panda to reach Europe alive

With the panda came feeding instructions to the effect that it should be given a quart of milk, with a little rice and grass each day. Bartlett felt that this diet was obviously inadequate and set

about changing it at once. Although the exhausted animal refused chicken, it readily accepted sweetened beef-tea and arrow-root or oatmeal porridge mixed with yolks of eggs. Soon it was strong enough to be let loose in the superintendent's garden and supplemented its diet with leaves, rose shoots and unripe apples. Above all it relished the yellow berries of *Pyrus vestita*. The panda, says Bartlett, "would grasp the branch with his paw, holding it tightly and bite off these berries one by one; so delighted with his food was he, that all other food was left as long as these berries lasted". Appropriately, the panda was commemorated in its official portrait

Red panda babies, born at Whipsnade Park in 1939. (*Fox Photos*)

using its forepaw to clutch its favourite food. The animal's manual dexterity aroused a great deal of interest, since, curiously enough, Brian Hodgson had never observed his captive specimens using their hands in this way.

At first the red panda had hardly lived up to its reputation for beauty, but as it became stronger it shed its old matted and ragged coat. Then a vividly coloured, lustrous new fur began to grow and its real glamour emerged at last. To hasten this process of transformation, Bartlett encouraged the animal to groom itself by spraying it every morning with a garden syringe. As far as the panda's temperament was concerned the improvement in its health brought about no change. Far from being sweet-natured and docile, as the world had been led to expect by Hodgson, it was bad-tempered, even ferocious at times, and refused to allow itself to be caressed. Bartlett wrote: "When offended, it would rush at me and strike with both feet, not like a cat, sideways or downwards, but forward, and the body raised like a bear, the claws projecting but not hooked or brought down like the claws of a cat; for although the claws are partly retractile, the animal cannot use them in that manner. At the moment of making the attack, it would utter a sharp spitting hiss . . ." No doubt this is why the lesser panda became popularly known as the "cat-bear" at the time.

Unusual and attractive though it was, the first "panda" to reach Europe did not produce any great impact on the animal-loving public at large. There were undoubtedly many reasons for this. It was not sufficiently dissimilar from a red fox or a raccoon and did not show itself to real advantage, being semi-nocturnal. But perhaps the most important factor was that its story ended abruptly and sadly, for it died suddenly during the night of 12th December 1869, without ever having had a real chance to capture a devoted human following. Its body was sent to the Royal College of Surgeons the next morning and there it came under the expert scalpel of William Henry Flower, Conservator of the Museum, who was delighted to have the opportunity to dissect such an interesting specimen. In 1870, Flower published a detailed paper about his findings that helped correct a number of inaccurate statements that had previously been made about the animal.

Zoologists were still puzzled, however, by the problem of exactly where the red panda should be placed in the classification of animal life. William Flower, and others, felt that it had sufficient peculiarities to merit being put in a distinct family. But how, exactly, should this family with its sole representative, the panda, be related to the other families of carnivores such as the raccoon group? In other words, which animals were the panda's closest relatives? Cautiously, Flower concluded, "This is a point which may still be left open for discussion. Some light will probably be thrown upon it when details are published of the structure of a remarkable new mammal lately obtained in Eastern Tibet by M. L'Abbé David . . ."

This remark proved to be prophetic. Unwittingly, since he believed that he had found a new kind of bear, the famous French priest and missionary, Père David, had, in fact, discovered another kind of panda, the giant panda as we know it today. In a sense, this is where our story really begins, for the beautiful and rare small red panda, which had held the stage for half a century, was about to be overshadowed by its more impressive black-and-white cousin from China. Nowadays, hardly anyone cares about the lesser panda, but there is hardly an infant alive who does not know and love the giant panda.

the giant panda
discovered

the giant panda discovered

CHAPTER TWO

The pelt of the giant panda

TODAY THE GIANT panda holds a secure position amongst the "Top Ten" animal favourites. We tend to take this climb to fame for granted, but in some respects it is rather unusual. One of the strangest aspects of the panda's success is that it lacks the traditional background of ancient mythology and legend so typical of the other great animal stars. For centuries, history and folk-lore have been enlivened by tales of fabulous elephants, winged horses, sacred monkeys and regal lions, but it is difficult to unearth more than a mere handful of references to the giant panda before Père David arrived on the scene in the nineteenth century.

Most people who write about the giant panda seem to feel obliged to provide something in the way of an historical background for it, no matter how second hand. They obviously feel that it is inconceivable that such a strange and striking creature should not have produced some reaction in a culture as civilized as that of China. To state blandly that the giant panda has been known to the Chinese since time immemorial may be the easiest way to dismiss the problem. It is undoubtedly true in a sense, but how well was the animal known and at what point was the inter-action between men and pandas first recorded?

The earliest instance we have discovered is given by J. H. Edgar, who mentions that this animal was included in the tribute of Yu from Liangchow, Szechuan, over 4,000 years ago. If this claim is justified then the suggestion is that before 2000 B.C. the panda, or, at least, its luxurious black-and-white pelt, was a sought-after commodity of great value. Since Liangchow lies in the giant panda's range, the statement certainly makes sense in geographical terms. On the question of antiquity, however, there is room for doubt. The orthodox list of Chinese rulers starts at the equivalent of 2852 B.C. If we accept this system of dating then the Emperor Yu is supposed to have reigned from 2205 to 2198 B.C. This also fits well, but unfortunately modern scholars are sceptical about the possibility of dating events accurately in this remote period of Chinese history when fact and legend were still confused.

The giant panda then fades from the scene until the seventh century A.D. when the bei-shung, or white bear, makes a more convincing historical debut. Willy Ley says that "Mention of this bei-shun is said to occur in Chinese chronicles as far back as our year 650 A.D.", while Ruth Harkness gives a slightly earlier date. In conversation with Arthur de Carle Sowerby, who was then Curator of the Shanghai Museum and an authority on pandas, she discovered that "The Chinese have known since the T'ang dynasty which began about A.D. 621, that this rare animal . . . lived in the mountains of far-western Szechuan, on the Tibetan border." Bernard Heuvelmans makes a similar claim; "As far as we know, the first mention of the bei-shung is in a manuscript dating from A.D. 621, during the reign of the first of the T'ang emperors." All this is rather vague, but a more elaborate account of seventh-century pandas is given by Herbert Wendt, who says; "A white bear from the mountainous bamboo forests of Yunnan province is already mentioned in a chronicle written in 621, during the reign of the first T'ang emperor. Then the Japanese imperial annals describe how, on October 22, 685 the Emperor of China sent the Tenno of Japan a gift of two living white bears and seventy white-bear skins. Thenceforth the pei-hsiung appears repeatedly in tax rolls, history and childrens' books."

Under the rule of the powerful T'ang emperors, whose dynasty spanned the period 618-907, China was the arbiter of the whole of Oriental Asia and combined political influence with intensive commercial activity. Trade flowed along the arteries of the "Silk Route" system, which linked the countries of Europe to central Asia and China, and one of these well-worn trails passed through panda country. Caravans carrying luxury merchandise over this particular route may well have acquired skins and even live specimens of the white bear, so enabling the emperor to make his lavish gesture. As these panda trophies were considered suitable gifts for a neighbouring ruler they must certainly have been highly prized. But the most astonishing feature of this story is the delivery of the two living animals to Japan. The transportation of pandas has proved a headache even in modern times. Given the difficulties of long distance travel in the seventh century it must have taken a major feat of animal husbandry to ensure that the Tenno's white bears reached their destination safely. What is more, this appears to be the first recorded occasion on which live giant pandas were exported from their native land.

This was a most notable event in panda history, providing the animals in question really were giant pandas. One intriguing suggestion which has been put forward is that the white bears were not giant pandas at all but were, in fact, polar bears, the snowy white giants of the Arctic, brought back from the North by Chinese hunters. In favour of this theory it can be argued that the polar bear is more common than the giant panda, so that seventy skins could be more easily assembled. Also, the polar bear is mentioned by Marco Polo in his travels, so that in the thirteenth century, at least, the Mongols must have known of it. If the Mongols had encountered it, then why not the ancient Chinese ?

Polar bear.
(Granada TV)

However, against the theory must be placed the fact that giant pandas live on Chinese soil, while polar bears are natives of the far north, thousands of miles away over inhospitable terrain. It is true that occasional sitings of the great Arctic bear have been made around the eastern coast of Siberia, and a few have actually penetrated south towards Japan, but these appear to be freak cases. They could hardly account for seventy skins.

In what quantities, or with what degree of regularity, white-bear skins found their way from the remote regions of the Tibetan borderland to the centre of Chinese civilization is uncertain. We must make a leap of a thousand years to find further mention of the bei-shung. David Crockett Graham, who spent many years working at the West China Union University in Chengtu, suggests that the Chinese certainly knew of the "white bear" in the seventeenth century. "During the Manchu dynasty skins of this animal were sent as tribute to the government of China by the aborigines of western Szechuan and eastern Tibet."

Assuming that the bei-shung skins mentioned in the early oriental records really came from giant pandas, why were they valued? They seem to have served two main purposes. Firstly the pelts made good sleeping mats. The fur on the giant panda's back is thick and woolly but, at the same time, wiry, so providing a dense yet springy surface when used as a mattress. Secondly, the bold, sharply defined black and white markings of the animal are very decorative, so panda skins were also used as ornamental rugs. Although it looks attractive, the fur is very coarse to the touch and was seldom, if ever, employed in the making of garments. This limits its uses considerably. For the experienced hunter, panda country is a paradise containing a number of animals whose skins have far more attractive qualities from the furriers' point of view.

Whatever its limitations, the pelt was the only part of the giant panda that seems to have had any economic importance at all. This could have been very little, given the difficulties of trapping the creature in its remote and impenetrable bamboo forests. In other respects, it was almost totally ignored. No mention of the bei-shung appears to have been made in the great Chinese *Materia Medica*, *Pen Ts'ao Kang Mu*, for instance. This work, written by Li Shih-chen, in 1597, contains a compilation of drugs made from animal materials. The author spent twenty-six years painstakingly cataloguing the whole traditional knowledge of drugs from China's remote past up to the sixteenth century. The omission of the bei-shung is surely significant, since the Chinese

大熊猫是我化成而不減其形古
又倫敦動物園自四川由邛彌來
三頭五年王延至身的點外並
圖片黑眼敗收至為明指有其最
特意公開示家送二為人士爭往觀
筆其性情之為和善全竹為生而
動作甚遲坡作時步水引人管
深金間想像其一生生活句為之圖
我可為吾國畫夹法一圖材料也

一九五九年五月六日蔣彝

*There are no early
pictures of giant pandas.
Paintings such as this
one by Chiang Yee are of
recent origin*

had a passion for using every conceivable animal ingredient for medicinal purposes.

There are several reasons why the giant panda may not have been included in the list. The obvious one is that the animal was not sufficiently well known or available as a potential therapeutic aid. Another possibility is that it was protected by religious sentiment. As a third alternative, it may have been too common to be considered worthy of attention. The evidence suggests that the giant panda was hardly sacred, since it was slaughtered by hunters. Moreover, any animal believed to have religious significance would surely have played some role in Chinese folk-lore and art. This would be equally expected if the giant panda was a very familiar creature, since common animals are invariably celebrated in this way. Yet the giant panda apparently made little, if any, impact either on oriental artists, or story-tellers. After a singularly unsuccessful search, for early giant panda pictures and legends, we consulted an expert from the Oriental Department of the British Museum, but he was unable to help us. He replied that "although an occasional skin may have reached Peking as tribute from the aboriginal tribes of Szechuan, this species was never sufficiently well-known to play any part in Chinese folk-lore. I have never seen any representation of it in Chinese painting or in bronzes or jades".

We can only conclude from this that in the more civilized regions of China, at least, the giant panda was virtually unknown in the past. The explanation appears to be largely connected with the fact that, as we have mentioned earlier, the geographical range of the species is restricted to remote and inhospitable areas of western China where the local inhabitants were no doubt bypassed by the mainstream of Chinese culture. Further east, giant pandas were virtually never seen in the flesh. They only appeared occasionally as sleeping mats, or rugs, acquired through trade or as tribute to the Chinese government, and in this disembodied form they were scarcely sufficiently stimulating to produce a crop of portraits or legends.

There is also another important point which must be taken into consideration when assessing why the Chinese neglected the giant panda, namely that, as far as they were concerned, the panda was just another kind of bear. Therefore, even if the giant panda was, in fact, better known than we have suggested, and Herbert Wendt really has good grounds for saying that it was a familiar character in oriental children's books from the seventh century onwards, it would simply have been amalgamated with the general bear image. In its homeland, the giant panda is known by several names, but they usually include the term for bear plus some descriptive word. Amongst its Chinese names are hsiung-maou (cat-bear), pei-hsiung or bei-shung (white bear), hua-hsiung (speckled bear) and ho shien (monk among bears). Superficially, bears and giant pandas are strikingly similar in appearance so it is easy to understand how the confusion arose. True the giant panda has very characteristic markings, but certain bears, including the Himalayan bear, which is comparable in size and whose range overlaps with that of the giant panda, have similar coloration. The main difference is that, whereas the Himalayan bear is basically black with a large off-white crescent on its chest, the giant panda has rather more white than black in its fur. But at what point is a black animal with white markings clearly distinguishable to the un-scientific eye from a white animal with black markings? There is also the added complication that in the Himalayas bordering on panda country there is a pale local race of the brown bear which almost qualifies as being white, since its coat is silvery-white with a creamy under-fur.

Judging by twentieth-century reports, we can be reasonably certain that in the past even people who inhabited panda territory itself often lived and died without ever setting eyes on the elusive

Himalayan black bear.
(Zool. Soc. London)

Pale form of the brown bear

Native spear trap

creature. Many of them were probably unaware that the animal existed. Others may have heard about it, but had no clear idea of what the giant panda looked like, and confused it with bears in general. Only the local hunters who made a living from the quarry which fell to their primitive fire-arms, or blundered into their spear-traps would have had any clear notion of the bei-shung. But to these men, struggling to survive in difficult and hostile country, the giant panda no doubt represented just another pelt in the bag. There is no evidence that they made a special point of hunting this animal. The traditional spear-trap was a device for taking not only giant pandas but any kind of large game. It consisted of a spear with an iron head wedged horizontally in the ground between two upright sticks, the tip of the weapon being set at an appropriate height to pierce the heart region of a large ungulate or bear. The device worked automatically, for a sapling was attached to the shaft of the spear and sprung by a trigger. From this a cord was run over the game's trail, so that when it was tampered with by a potential quarry, the spear, guided by the upright sticks, was driven forward with tremendous impetus and plunged into the animal's body. The giant panda skins recorded in tax rolls in ancient times were presumably part of the random haul gathered by these effective, but non-selective traps. Given the inferior quality of giant panda fur, it is even possible that their pelts were not over-enthusiastically received by the Chinese government, except in so much as they were considered unusual and rare.

If this then was the situation in China, small wonder that the white bear aroused little interest in the West before its official discovery in 1869. Few people knew that the creature existed and among scholarly circles it was either dismissed as a fanciful legend, or thought to be just another type of bear. The most popular theory, as we have already noted, was that the Chinese bei-shung, being reputedly white, must be a polar bear, the only well-known white species. This suggests that westerners were unfamiliar with skins of the animal, since the black patches in its coat are too striking to be over-looked. However, melanistic polar bears, not to mention partial albino black bears, are not beyond the bounds of biological possibility. If the odd giant panda pelt had reached Europe through trade, or missionaries, it could have been explained as an unusual bear mutation. Or the pelt may have been thought to belong to some ordinary domestic animal since, due to selective breeding by man, black and white markings are very characteristic of many domestic species. Superficially, there is nothing remarkable about the actual quality of giant panda's fur that would have distinguished it from either the zoologist's or the furrier's point of view.

There is a fascinating rumour that a living bei-shung actually reached Paris during the eighteenth century. Unfortunately, the author who reports that this is said to have happened was unable to recall the source of his information. We, too, have been unable to locate it. If a giant panda had reached Europe in those days, it also may have passed for a freak bear, so disappearing from the pages of history leaving scarcely a trace. Yet the story seems highly improbable. The eighteenth century was a golden era for the study of animal anatomy and one imagines the French zoologists hovering like vultures around any strange specimen, competing anxiously to pounce on its corpse and carry it off to their dissecting tables.

As late as the middle of the nineteenth century, the rich plant and animal life of China was still largely unexplored. About this time military pressure from the European nations forced the Celestial Empire to open up to foreign penetration. The position of missionaries and traders became rather more secure and both expanded their spheres of activity. Now Europeans were given their first glimpse of the wonderful flora and fauna of such remote areas as Mongolia and Szechuan through the efforts of French Catholic missionary priests and, notably, the pioneer work of Abbé Armand David.

This remarkable man combined intense religious devotion with a passionate interest in natural history. He wrote on one occasion, "I passionately love the beauties of nature; the marvels of the hand of God transport me with such admiration that in comparison the finest work of man seems only trivial." Even as a young boy he showed a keen enthusiasm for his favourite subject. Guided and encouraged by his father, Fructueux Dominique, a doctor and eminent citizen of the little town of Espelette in the Basses-Pyrénées, David browsed through scholarly books on natural history and collected butterflies and insects in the mountains around his home. But his main ambition was to become a priest and, in 1850, he took his vows in the order of St. Vincent de Paul whose missionaries were known as Lazarists. As early as 1852, while teaching at a college on the Italian Riviera he wrote to his superior that he dreamed of Chinese missions and it was for this reason that he had become a priest in the Lazarist order. Ten years passed, however, before he was ordained a missionary and set sail for China. Before he left, he had been commissioned by the authorities of the Museum of Natural History in Paris to collect botanical and zoological material. This he proceeded to do soon after his arrival in Peking and so impressed the Museum's director, Henri Milne-Edwards, with the excellence of his specimens that it was arranged for Abbé David to undertake special scientific work, sponsored by the French government.

Père David, as he is usually known in scientific literature, was stationed in China from 1862 to 1874 and during this period undertook three important journeys for the Museum of Natural History. The scientific discoveries that he made ensured his undying fame as a naturalist and explorer. The earnest, black-haired, keen-eyed missionary, who had gone to China "pursued with the thought of dying while working at the saving of infidels", returned home convinced that, at the current rate of progress, it would be forty or fifty thousand years before the Celestial Empire would be wholly Christian. He himself, however, was not destined to become a martyr in that cause and survived not only religious persecution, but bandits, the severe hardships of travel, inadequate food and severe illness. The last twenty-six years of his life were spent mostly in Paris as a celebrity honoured throughout the scientific world. By then, a handsome white-haired old man he entertained his friends with vivid accounts of his adventures and the marvels he had seen. Although modest, he had a sense of

Père Armand David in
Chinese dress

humour and a flair for dramatic effects. Just before his death in 1900, at the age of seventy-four, he made a point of carrying around with him a huge pet spider which he is said to have trained to run back to him on the word of command.

Père David's fame was well deserved for, during his stay in China, he had sent back to Europe a vast collection of plants and introduced many lovely new species now familiar in our gardens. He discovered fifty-eight birds new to science, about a hundred new insects and many mammals. The latter included the extraordinary snub-nosed Roxellana monkey and the milou, now known as Père David's deer, a curious creature, extinct in the wild, but lingering on the Imperial Park at Peking. Many plants and animals were named after the French priest, yet ironically his most important discovery of all does not bear his name. This animal was, of course, the giant panda.

The discovery was made during his second journey which took him to Szechuan and the independent principalities of western China and lasted from 26th May 1868 to 25th July 1870. On each of his three major collecting trips, Père David kept a diary which he filled with copious notes recording his impressions and scientific data that would help him later in writing up his collections. These field journals were all published, apparently with little editing or revision, and their lively on-the-spot flavour is retained in print. The diary of the second journey, so momentous in giant panda history, appeared under the title *Journal d'un Voyage dans le centre de la Chine et dans le Tibet Oriental*, in the form of Bulletins appended to the Nouvelles Archives du Muséum d'Histoire Naturelle de Paris, in 1872, 1873 and 1874.

Unfortunately, it is impossible to tell from his diary whether Père David deliberately set out to look for the Chinese bei-shung, or whether he stumbled upon it almost by accident. We know that he was encouraged to go to the western frontiers of China by reports from fellow missionaries who assured him that there were many interesting animals to be found in the high mountains which had escaped the deforestation that invariably accompanied Chinese agricultural expansion. On 16th June 1868, he met, in Shanghai, a Chinese who was formerly a pupil of the missionary college in Moupin. The director of this institution, M. Arnal, was already engaged in preparing many interesting new birds and mammals to be sent to France, but the task was a huge one. Père David wrote, "This young man tells me that, although M. Arnal's researches have lasted two years, his hunters have not succeeded in procuring all the animals living in the woods of Muping. So

A typical view of giant panda country (From *Nat. Hist. Mag., N.Y.*)

there will still be some gleanings for me, at least among less remarkable species."

Had David been told of the white bear before setting off on the long and uncomfortable boat trip up the Yangtze River, past the dangerous rapids to Chungking, on 13th October 1868? Or did he learn of the creature from missionaries in Chungking itself when he arrived there, more than six weeks later, weary and travel-worn? From Chungking he pressed on to Chengtu, the ancient walled city which for years had been an outpost of the caravan trade where, again, he gleaned as much information as possible about the zoological treasures to be found in the nearby mountains. On the eve of departure from Chengtu he obviously felt gloomy and rather sceptical and wrote in his diary, "I am busy preparing my numerous pieces of baggage to leave tomorrow and, if it please God, spend a year in Muping, the promised land where everyone has said there are marvels. I admit, however, that I am not enthusiastic, knowing how often I have been misled by Chinese promises."

By 1st March he had reached Moupin and was comfortably installed in the Catholic college there. This teaching establishment had been founded fifty or sixty years before, when persecutions in China had obliged the missionaries to seek refuge in the independent kingdom of the prince of the Man-tzu. Père David noted that the people living in the inaccessible mountains of this tiny barbarian state made a meagre living from gathering medicinal herbs, hunting, and making potash. In type and language they differed considerably from the Chinese, for whom he had little admiration and seldom a good word. He was therefore saddened to observe that, even in Moupin, "the industrious, increasing population of the Celestial Empire is penetrating quickly and taking possession of the land under one pretext or another, and will end by having its customs, language, costume, and also its faults adopted. A few years ago no Chinese had access to Muping. Now they are to be found throughout the principality". But Père David did not spend long pondering on this unhappy state of affairs, he had important work to do. He hastily set about collecting specimens and made arrangements with local hunters to bring him some large mammals. Acquiring material through these contacts proved to be expensive and he noted resentfully that the hunters demanded five or six times the normal prices. Certain

Père David

bans were imposed on hunting by the prince of the district, super-ficially, at least, on religious grounds. These the poverty-stricken inhabitants were willing to flout, but they expected to be well re-warded for their pains.

The very first mention of the giant panda comes under Père David's entry in his diary for 11th March 1869. It was a beautiful sunny day and the priest, accompanied by a student, had gone on an expedition into the lower valleys of Hong-chan-tin in quest of specimens. "On returning from our excursion we are invited to rest at the home of a certain Li, the principal landowner in the valley, who entertains us with tea and sweet-meats. At this pagan's I see a fine skin of the famous white and black bear (du fameux ours blanc et noir), which appears to be fairly large. It is a very remarkable species and I rejoice when I hear my hunters say that I shall certainly obtain the animal within a short time. They tell me that they will go out as early as tomorrow to kill this carnivore which it seems must constitute an interesting novelty for science."

From the way that Père David describes this incident we can only infer that he already knew of the famous black-and-white bear. But we know from his diary that he had already met a hunter called Li who was presumably his host on 11th March. The interesting question is whether David recognized the pelt at once or whether he learnt what it was from the landowner. He in-variably questioned people he met about the animals of the dis-trict, and it was possibly as a result of this, that Li produced his handsome skin and explained to the foreigner that it belonged to the famous bei-shung which lived in the Hsifan Mountains. Whether Père David had heard it mentioned before or not, he would have found out as much as he could about the creature and made every effort to obtain a specimen to send back to Paris. He did not realize that the animal was quite unique or call it a giant panda but, even as a remarkable species of bear, it was sufficiently interesting to the zoological world.

On 23rd March, he wrote, "My Christian hunters return today after a ten-day absence. They bring me a young white bear, which they took alive but unfortunately killed so it could be carried more easily." Since he regarded himself as a follower of St. Francis, David deplored the unnecessary taking of animal life and always regretted having to kill animals in order to prepare specimens. Yet, dead or alive, the young animal fascinated him as a naturalist. He continues, "The young white bear, which they sell to me very dearly, is all white except the four limbs, ears, and around the eyes, which are deep black. The colours are the same as those of the adult's skin which I examined the other day at the home of Li, the hunter. This must, therefore, be a new species of *Ursus*, which is very remarkable not only for its colour, but also because of its paws which are hairy underneath, and for other characters." Père David's conviction that the animal must be a new species of bear was further confirmed when on 1st April, "They bring me a white bear which they tell me is fully adult. Its colours are exactly the same as those of the young one that I have already, only the black is less pure and the white more soiled. The animal's head is very big and the muzzle round and short instead of being pointed as in the Pekin bear."

Père David did not delay in informing his friends in Paris of his discovery. A description of the animal, which he named *Ursus melanoleucus* (black-and-white bear), was sent to Professor Alphonse Milne-Edwards, son and, later, successor of the director of the Paris Natural History Museum. In a letter from Moupin, dated 21st March 1869, David explained that he was forwarding a collection of specimens but, knowing that the shipment would not arrive in France for a long time, requested that the description of the new bear should be published immediately. It did, in fact, appear in the Museum's Bulletin of the same year and read as follows: "*Ursus melanoleucus* A.D. Very large according to my hunters. Ears short. Tail very short. Hair fairly short; beneath the four feet very hairy. Colours: white, with the ears, the surroundings of the eyes, the tip of the tail and the four legs brownish black. The black on the forelegs is joined over the back in a straight band. I have just received a young bear of this kind and I have seen the mutilated skins of adult specimens. The colours are always the same and equally distributed. I have not seen this species, which is easily the prettiest kind of animal I know, in the museums of Europe. Is it possible that it is new to science? For the past twenty days I have employed more than ten hunters to capture some old specimens of this remarkable bear." A postscript is then added to this brief description. "April 4—An adult female of the black-and-white bear has just come into my possession. The coat is yellowish and the black is darker and shinier than in the young specimen."

When Père David's specimens reached Paris, Alphonse Milne-Edwards naturally paid particular attention to the remarkable Chinese bear. But after a detailed examination of skins and skeletons he realized that his friend David had been wrong in identifying the creature as a bear, although he felt that at first sight any naturalist might have mistaken it for one. In an article entitled, "Sur quelques Mammifères du Tibet Oriental", published in 1870, Milne-Edwards wrote: "In its external form, indeed, it very much resembles a Bear, but the osteological characters and the dental system clearly distinguish it from the Bears and come nearer to the Pandas and Raccoons. It must constitute a new genus which I have called *Ailuropoda*."

Later when he found that the scientific name *Ailuropoda* had already been used in a different context, the French zoologist modified it to *Ailuropus*. The name was originally selected to recall the resemblance between the feet of the newly discovered carnivore and those of *Ailurus*, the lesser panda, the only animal known as a panda in those days. So, during the nineteenth century, the full scientific title of the animal, which we know today as the giant panda, was *Ailuropus melanoleucus*, or the "panda-like black-and-white animal." Later taxonomists changed the name back again to Milne-Edward's original suggestion and the giant panda is known today as *Ailuropoda melanoleuca* meaning, literally, "black-and-white panda-foot".

On the many occasions when Père David referred to "the most important zoological discovery I have been given to make", he was repeatedly obliged to mention that his name *Ursus melanoleucus* had been dropped because it was misleading. Yet, unlike certain other scientists, he accepted Milne-Edward's new name for his greatest discovery. Perhaps he sometimes felt annoyed with himself for failing to spot the relationship between his "bear" and the lesser panda, particularly as he had obtained specimens of both within a short space of time and had noticed that there were similarities between their heads and feet. With a flash of genius his good friend Milne-Edwards had pin-pointed the connection, but this the unassuming priest accepted with considerable good grace.

While Alphonse Milne-Edwards was busily writing up his anatomical evidence to substantiate his classification, Père David, in December 1871, gave a report to his sponsors, the scientific administrators of the Natural History Museum. It was published the next year and included the first description of the habits of the giant panda in the wild. Brief as it was, his information is well worth mention. He wrote: "This animal which the hunters call Paé-shioung (white bear) is very much rarer than the black Tibetan bear, which inhabits the same forests; it stays much higher and appears to have a vegetable diet. But, nevertheless, it does not refuse flesh when the occasion presents itself; and I even think that this is its principal food in winter, a season in which it is not

inclined to remain asleep." It is interesting that Père David did not record the giant panda as an exclusive bamboo-eater. As we shall see, later authors frequently did so. We know now that Père David was right and they were wrong, although he went too far when he suggested that in winter the animal was predominantly carnivorous.

The first detailed account of the anatomy of the giant panda, together with an attractive portrait and six other plates showing the bony structure, appeared in 1874. It was part of Alphonse Milne-Edward's contribution to the monumental work on the natural history of mammals which he published in conjunction with his father, Henri, between 1868 and 1874, under the title *Recherches pour servir a l'histoire naturelle des Mammifères.*" Bone by bone and tooth by tooth, the younger Milne-Edwards analysed minutely the ways in which the "Ailurope", as he called the giant panda, resembled or differed from other carnivores. The giant panda's penultimate molar caused him grave concern because of its similarities with the equivalent tooth in certain fossil pachyderms, but he concluded that, "nevertheless, it is between the Bears and the Pandas that the Ailurope must take its place in our methodical classification". One quite unique feature of the giant panda, the "sixth claw", which we know today assists the animal in grasping bamboo stems with its front paws, did not escape Milne-Edwards' thorough eye, although he makes no suggestion about its possible function. He mentions that, whereas the back feet of *Ailuropus* have "a row of five little fleshy pin-cushions" at the base of the toes, on the front feet there is an extra "fleshy pin-cushion, without hairs, near the heel". On the basis of all the anatomical evidence at his disposal the French zoologist believed that *Ailuropus* constituted a separate genus more valid than many of the other genera in the Order Carnivora.

Yet, although the giant panda was now officially "known to science", for many years to come it still remained very much a creature of mystery. It came to be popularly known as the "clawed bear", or the "bamboo bear" and some scientists thought that "harlequin bear" would be a suitable common name. In other words, the giant panda was still widely regarded as a bear. At the turn of the century a specimen at the British Museum was still being exhibited as a "parti-coloured bear".

About the same time the German zoologist Max Weber undertook a general re-classification of the mammals and pronounced that the *bambushbär* (bamboo bear), far from being related to the lesser panda and the raccoon, as Milne-Edwards had suggested, was in fact a living fossil, the last remaining ally of *Hyaenarctos*, a hyaena-sized Miocene carnivore. Weber believed *Hyaenarctos* to be a primeval vegetarian bear and therefore decided that *Ailuropoda melanoleuca* must be an ancestral bear which, by some fluke, had survived into modern times.

Even today, controversy over the exact classification of the giant panda still rages, although the animal is much better known than it was barely a century ago. Then, the whole of zoological knowledge about this particular species rested on just a few specimens in the museums of Europe. There were four examples in the Natural History Museum of Paris, obtained through Père David, and one other in the museum of Stuttgart, in Germany, which was acquired some time later. This fifth specimen was apparently purchased from a hunter in panda country by a Chinese merchant who then traded it to a German.

A scant handful of mounted specimens could hardly be expected to advance knowledge of the giant panda to any degree, but one unsolved historical riddle remains. Is it possible that several live giant pandas actually reached Europe in the nineteenth century? Several authors have claimed that they did. We have heard that there is also a rumour to this effect circulating in Paris at the

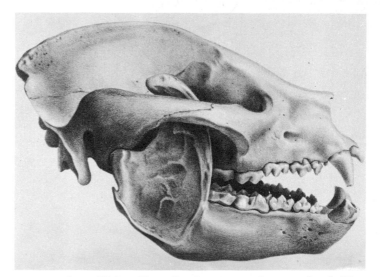

The skull of the giant panda. (From *Milne-Edwards*)

present time. Helen Fox, for instance, who translated Père David's diaries into English under the auspices of Harvard University and published the results as *Père David's Diary* in 1949, implies that there were live giant pandas in Paris in the nineteenth century. In the introduction to the book she writes: "Among the animals discovered by Abbé David, the giant panda, *Ailuropoda melanoleuca*, created the greatest interest. It can be imagined what a stir was caused when the panda arrived at the Jardin d'Acclimatation. For a while it was the only example in Europe; but the first to come did not long survive its transference from the mountains of Szechuan."

Could this have been the adult female that the local hunters brought Père David on 1st April 1869 ? In his diary he does not mention whether the animal was alive or dead. True, it seems unlikely that the hunters would take the trouble to bring back a live adult from the mountains when a young one had provided them with such a transport problem that they killed it. But the possibility remains that the priest gave them sufficient financial reward for the young specimen to encourage them to try and trap a live giant panda for him.

In 1951, Jessie Dobson, Curator of the Hunterian Museum at the Royal College of Surgeons in London, published a paper in the Proceedings of the Zoological Society of London which also suggests that Père David was instrumental in obtaining live giant pandas for the Paris Zoo. Her main subject was the discovery of Père David's deer, but she also refers briefly to the French priest's interest in the "white bear" that was said to live in the mountains of western China. After describing how local hunters obtained a young giant panda for Père David, she adds, "For convenience of

41

transport, this specimen had to be killed, but later several others were obtained alive and sent to Paris. (In 1888 the Jardin des Plantes had four Giant Pandas, the only examples outside China.)" Miss Dobson's story has been elaborated by later authors so that the implication is that the few living specimens of the giant panda which Père David organized to send home were on display in the Paris Zoo for a number of years.

The authorities at the Jardin des Plantes and Natural History Museum in Paris have not, unhappily, been able to give us any further information about this fascinating story. Moreover, Miss Dobson is unable to trace her notes which, apparently, contained a great deal of information from original sources. She is convinced that her claim is based on sound evidence, if only it could be located. The contributions of Père David himself throw no further light on the subject. In a paper presented in 1888 on *La Faune Chinoise*, which was published a year later, he simply states that only four museum examples of *Ailuropus* existed at that time and all of these he had brought back from Moupin. It seems rather strange that he did not mention the fact that some of these animals were still breathing, if, in fact, there were living examples in Paris at the time. Also, would these not have been housed in the Zoo rather than in the Paris Museum which was devoted to dead specimens? We cannot eliminate the intriguing possibility that living giant pandas set foot on European soil before the twentieth century, even if the stress of the journey and lack of knowledge of their needs cut their stay to a very short one. Unless new evidence comes to light, however, we feel obliged to adhere to the traditional story that all Père David's specimens were dead on arrival in France, and that many years were to pass after his original discovery before scientists, or the public, had a chance to study the extraordinary animal in the flesh.

We feel that perhaps there has been some confusion between the arrival of giant pandas and lesser pandas in Europe in the late nineteenth century. The small red panda, *Ailurus fulgens*, then itself a rare and sensational animal, was known as *the* panda ever since Frédéric Cuvier gave it that popular name in 1825, whereas its big cousin, the giant panda, despite Milne-Edwards' efforts, was still generally known as a bear.

The giant panda was so little known that, in the 1890s, the English zoologist E. Ray Lankester, was thrilled when his friend, Professor Alphonse Milne-Edwards, sent him a cast of the skull "of the remarkable bear-like animal brought home from Tibet by Père David". On being appointed Director of the Natural History

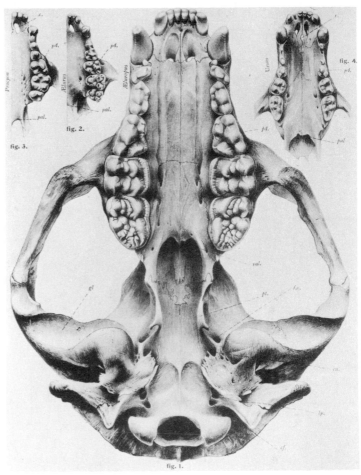

The skull of the giant panda compared with those of (left to right, top) the raccoon, red panda and bear. (From Lankester)

Department of the British Museum in 1898, Lankester looked up the material "relating to *Aeluropus* in the Collection, and was much pleased to find that, in addition to a fine skull and mounted skin, the Museum possessed certain of the limb-bones and incomplete feet of *Aeluropus*, obtained in 1896." These odd bones, discovered tucked away in one of the countless cupboards of his new domain, excited Lankester much more than the spectacular skin. (We know that in the 1890s the British Museum was enriched by the remains of two pandas. One of these specimens was secured by the Russian explorers Berezovski and Potanin and the other, a male, was captured by the local hunters employed by F. W. Styan in Yangliupa in north-western Szechuan. Probably it was the former specimen which Lankester unearthed so unexpectedly.)

The new Director of the Natural History Department of the British Museum had already decided, after studying his panda skull cast at Oxford, that, despite the claims of certain other eminent zoologists, it differed greatly from the skull of any bear and in certain respects came close to that of the lesser panda. The foot and leg bones which he discovered at the British Museum only confirmed his opinion "that in very important and distinctive points *Aeluropus* agrees with *Aelurus*, and *Procyon* (more closely with the former) and differs widely from *Ursus*." In other words, Lankester, like his colleague Milne-Edwards, felt that the giant panda was much more closely related to the red panda, and to a lesser degree the raccoon, than to the bears. One of the principal opponents of this theory was Richard Lydekker, whom Lankester consulted before taking action on his decision. In a paper addressed to the Linnean Society on 21st February 1901, the then Director of the British Museum describes what followed. "Having satisfied myself on these points, I requested Mr. Lydekker, who had not previously examined the limb-bones of *Aeluropus*, to go over the specimens and give me the result of his observations. He entirely accepted my conclusion that *Aeluropus* must be removed from association with the Bears, and associated with *Aelurus* and *Procyon*. It has accordingly been removed to that position in the exhibition gallery of the Museum, and is no longer to be spoken of as 'the parti-coloured bear', but as 'the great panda'."

For the first time, the giant panda was exhibited under a name very similar to the one by which it is known throughout the English-speaking word today. It was described as the great and later as the giant panda in order to differentiate it from its smaller relative, now known as the lesser or red panda. The new popular name caught on rapidly and no doubt inspired the western zoologists and trophy-hunters who went to China in quest of the rare and beautiful animal. Soon the peace of the giant panda's mountainous bamboo-forest retreat was to be shattered by intrepid Europeans and Americans eager to be put on record as the first westerners to shoot the mysterious and retiring "giant", and to glorify their local museum with a stuffed exhibit of the elusive prize.

Chinese symbol for giant panda

the panda killers

the panda killers

CHAPTER THREE

*Impenetrable bamboo
jungle in Wassuland*

FOR MANY DECADES the giant panda remained one of the rarest animals known to man, despite the invasions of panda country that followed its discovery. A few specimens, trapped by local hunters and purchased by western explorers or missionaries, found their way into museums outside China, but for a long time the animal eluded all the foreigners who tried to shoot it. As a result, it became the most challenging animal trophy on earth.

True, most of the expeditions that went to the wilds of Szechuan were by no means designed exclusively as panda hunts. The cost of such specialized ventures would have been far too high and the chances of success too remote. Finances were available, however, for expeditions of a more comprehensive type. For instance, thirty years or so after Père David discovered the giant panda, Britain and America sent new explorers to China whose task was to repeat his scientific work under more favourable conditions. Amongst these botanists and zoologists were Ernest H. Wilson and Walter Zappey. When in west-central Szechuan they saw very definite signs of the giant panda and noticed that it had beaten tracks through the thickets, "frequenting the same haunts for long periods, as is evident from the large heaps of its dung which are often met with in the Bamboo jungle." Wilson recorded various pieces of information which he gleaned from the local inhabitants and noted that the animals fed exclusively on bamboo shoots. He wrote: "The young shoots which continue to spring up from June to the end of September, according to the altitude and species, are white within and excellent eating. The Giant Panda shows good taste in confining his diet to this excellent vegetable!" Yet, while combing the animal's homeland for plant and animal treasure, neither Wilson, nor any of his fellow scientists, caught so much as a glimpse of the panda itself.

So powerful was the allure of the mysterious panda that it sometimes proved fatal. One unfortunate explorer, Lieutenant J. W. Brooke, was murdered in 1910 by the Lolos, the strange and often inhospitable people who inhabited remote areas where giant pandas were to be found. Later, his widow presented to the British Museum a giant panda skin that her husband had purchased while in Szechuan.

There is some controversy as to who could claim to be the first westerner to actually see a living panda in the wild. One contender for this particular honour was Brigadier-General G. E. Pereira, an Englishman who made many contributions to zoological knowledge by way of new animal discoveries. He longed to kill a panda and kept a sharp watch for it while on his various expeditions through Western China and Eastern Tibet. His ambition was never fulfilled and he even failed to find so much as a trace of the animal in local tales. Then, one magical day, for a brief moment he saw a furry white animal perched in a distant tree which may just possibly have been a giant panda. In 1916, J. H. Edgar had a similar experience. While travelling in wild country near Kinsha he spotted a large white animal curled up in the fork of an oak tree. Being unarmed at the time he did not dare approach any nearer than a hundred yards, so we shall never know for certain whether the sleeping giant was a panda or not.

At last, after nearly fifty years of frustration for panda-seekers, another naturalist, like Père David, held a giant panda in his arms. But there was a difference—this young animal was alive. The lucky zoologist was a German called Hugo Weigold, a member of the Stoetzner expedition to West China and Eastern Tibet that took place during World War I. His personal attempts at panda hunting yielded nothing, although being an athletic person he took part in a number of strenuous native hunts. The technique used was to put dogs on to a fresh trail and then follow their lead at top speed, hoping to catch up with the animal and shoot it. The nearest Weigold came to seeing his quarry was a flurry of waving branches as the animal fled from its pursuers. None the less, he was given an opportunity to study a giant panda in the flesh in its homeland.

While in the province of Wassu, east of the Min River, in 1916, he bought a giant panda from the local inhabitants. Unfortunately, it was a baby "bamboo bear", as the panda was popularly known in Germany, and despite Weigold's loving attempts to hand rear it, died after a very short time for lack of the right kind of food. This is the official story anyway, although there are rumours that the animal was killed shortly after it was brought in by Chinese hunters. In any case, this particular episode in the panda story was not generally known in America or Britain, no doubt on account of the war. Nor was the fact that the expedition secured no less than five other specimens, the skins of three adult males and one female together with their complete or incomplete skulls, and a skin minus any bones. These specimens were eventually sent to the Berlin Museum, although the infant panda, at least, appears to have been first displayed at Dresden where Weigold held an academic post during this period.

The Stoetzner expedition proved conclusively that the giant panda was by no means extinct, as certain scientists were beginning to fear. It still survived in the remote Hsifan Mountains, if nowhere else. For the big game hunters, in particular, it remained a supreme challenge, for as yet no westerner had experienced the thrill of personally shooting one. All past experiences had shown that this rare and beautiful Chinese prey was incredibly difficult to locate in the flesh, but soon the chase was on again.

Undaunted by the problems involved, brothers Colonel Theodore and Kermit Roosevelt, sons of the famous American President and ardent big game hunter Teddy Roosevelt, laid a daring plan. They would undertake a hunting expedition to Indo-China and West China proper with the killing of a giant panda as their main goal. Indeed, they swore that they would not return home until they had shot a panda. Since it was led by two such prominent Americans, the Roosevelt Expedition was naturally widely publicized and the world waited with eager anticipation to see whether they would fulfil their boast.

Before setting off for the East in 1928, the Roosevelts consulted experts and gleaned every scrap of information available about the special characteristics and likely whereabouts of the giant panda. In so far as possible, nothing was left to chance. The expedition had sound backing, for it was sponsored by the Chicago Field

The members of the famous Roosevelt expedition. From left to right: Jack Young, Herbert Stevens, Theodore Roosevelt, Philip Tao and Suydam Cutting. (From Nat. Hist. Mag., N.Y.)

Museum of Natural History and financed by William V. Kelly, one of the Museum's patrons. The other members of the party were selected with great care and included Suydam Cutting, the Tibetan explorer, and Jack Young, a New York born Chinese big game hunter, who we shall meet again later in our story. Only one real problem remained. What was to be done if only one giant panda presented itself as a target? This the Roosevelts solved by agreeing in advance that if one of them sighted the beast both brothers would fire simultaneously so that they might share the unique honour of being the first white man to kill a giant panda.

When the expedition arrived at its destination, the rugged mountains of the lonely borderland between China and Tibet, it found the provinces of Yunnan and Szechuan devastated by bandits and terrorized in particular by an outlaw leader named Chang Chi Pa, the "stutterer". This ex-muleteer had a sinister reputation for cruelty and had recently tortured a lama by suspending him from a tree by his thumbs and weighting his feet with rocks. Apart from such perils, the country itself presented other hazards from the hunter's point of view. Kermit Roosevelt wrote later: "The parts of Yunnan and Szechuan through which we passed can by no stretch of the imagination be termed a big game paradise. It is no country for the inexperienced hunter nor for one who wishes to secure a large bag without undue expenditure of time and effort."

The giant panda was, of course, the first prize which this wild terrain had to offer, if only it were possible to find one. One obvious way to go about this was to question the local inhabitants, but as Kermit Roosevelt lamented: "Native information required careful checking, for even after a detailed description of the animal, accompanied by a showing of a plate depicting it, we could not rely on a native's word as to its presence in a district. Sometimes this was due to very hazy notions of coloration and the assumption that the white crescent on the black bear's chest entitled it to be called a bei-shung. At other times misinformation was wilful, whether with the common impulse to give pleasant and agreeable news or because the native counted on earning some money as guide before his deception would be discovered."

Given this situation, the members of the American expedition came to mistrust all local information and to rely on more concrete evidence for guidance in their search. Secretive though it might be, the giant panda invariably left behind obvious clues in the shape of copious droppings that could easily be identified owing to the animal's unusual diet of bamboo shoots and stalks. Using such signs, the party first came across indubitable evidence of its quarry in Moupin country in Szechuan. It was now March and the mountains were covered with deep snow so that the animal's tracks also betrayed its former presence. The Roosevelts were convinced that given a good pack of bear hounds, of the type available in the United States, the coveted giant panda would be within their grasp. Unfortunately all they managed to muster in the way of canine support was a group of small wiry local dogs each accompanied by its master. These dogs proved a distinct disappointment for "their sense of smell was quite evidently only fair, and we felt that their value lay in perhaps starting an animal, and driving him up a tree". The odds against their being able to shoot a giant panda under these conditions seemed too great and so the Roosevelts decided to try their luck elsewhere.

Despite warnings of danger from the Chinese authorities and Western missions, the intrepid hunters ventured into Lololand, still an almost legendary district in those days. But instead of being murdered or enslaved by these intriguing people, after an initial period of coolness and veiled suspicion, they received hospitality and help. The Lolos said that they knew of the giant panda but it was extremely rare. They themselves only killed the animal to protect their beehives, which it raided occasionally, but in general regarded it as a semi-divinity.

Slender as its chances seemed, the party did not give up hope

Artist's impression of the "savage challenge" to be met by the panda hunters. (Nat. Hist. Mag., N.Y.)

The snow covered slopes of the giant panda mountains. (From *Nat. Hist. Mag., N.Y.*)

and soon its optimism was rewarded. The Roosevelts described the ultimate triumph in their book *Trailing the Giant Panda*, which was published in New York in 1929. "On the morning of the 13th of April we came upon giant panda tracks in the snow near Yehli, south of Tchienlu in the Hsifan Mountains. The animal had evidently passed a goodish while before the snow ceased falling, but some sign that one of the Lolos found proved to be recent enough to thoroughly arouse all four natives. . . We had been following the trail for two-and-a-half hours when we came to a more open jungle. Unexpectedly close I heard a clicking chirp. One of the Lolo hunters darted forward. He had not gone forty yards before he turned back to eagerly motion to us to hurry. As I gained his side he pointed to a giant spruce thirty yards away.

Native hunters with their dogs. (From *Animal Kingdom, N.Y.*)

The bole was hollowed, and from it emerged the head and forequarters of a bei-shung. He looked sleepily from side to side as he sauntered forth and walked slowly away into the bamboos. As soon as Ted came up we fired simultaneously at the outline of the disappearing panda. Both shots took effect. He was a splendid old male, the first that the Lolos had any record of as being killed in this Yehli region. Our great good fortune could only with much effort be credited. After holding aloof, the Hunting Gods had turned about and brewed the unusual chain of circumstances that alone could enable us to shoot a giant panda, trailing him without dogs and with the crowning bit of luck that permitted us to fire jointly."

News of the death of this inoffensive panda, so rudely interrupted at his siesta, flashed around the world. At the time the killing was regarded as a splendid feather in the sporting Roosevelts' cap, although Kermit Roosevelt himself admitted that the animal had put up no resistance. In a scientific article published a year after his book and illustrated by a plate showing a remarkably sombre and surly looking beast, he says that: "The giant panda, from all we could learn is not a savage animal. After the shooting, our Kashmir shikarries remarked that he was a sahib, a gentleman, for when hit he had remained silent, and had not called out as does a bear." Equally he had no qualms about acknowledging that the animal was extremely rare and, strange as it may seem to us today with our great preoccupation with the problem of animal conservation, he felt that this only added to the expedition's achievement.

When the success of the Kelly-Roosevelt expedition was announced everyone was delighted, including the zoologists, who felt that this was a definite contribution to scientific knowledge. They were still worried about how the giant panda should be classified taxonomically. For instance, when one of the Roosevelt brothers had sought the advice of Royal Pocock, a former superintendent of the London Zoo, before setting off for China, the Englishman had begged him to try and obtain a certain anatomical structure, if he did shoot one, "to settle finally the point at issue in its classification". Pocock was anxious to show that the giant panda was definitely related to the lesser panda and not to the bears or the raccoon family. The vital piece of evidence which interested him so much was apparently the giant panda's genitals, although he is rather coy on this subject. Roosevelt did not disappoint him for, as Pocock explained some time later, "On his return to London, he told me how he had shot a specimen, skinned it, took such parts as were wanted for mounting for the Chicago Museum, and made his way back to camp, his attendants carrying the spoils, but forgot all about my request. Just however, as he was settling down for the night, the recollection of it flashed across his mind; and, fearing lest jungle scavengers should destroy what was left of the carcass before daylight, he roused a couple of his men and, tired as he was, retraced his steps to the spot by lantern light and recovered the 'missing link'."

The skin of the Roosevelts' fully grown male panda was sent back to the United States with another specimen which the expedition obtained from local hunters, to be stuffed and displayed with pride in the Field Museum. Chicago's panda exhibit aroused the envy of other American museums and produced a rash of explorers all anxious to emulate the Roosevelts' example. The Philadelphia Academy of Natural Sciences, determined that the second giant panda to be killed by westerners should end up in its own exhibition halls, prepared a full-scale expedition to Western Szechuan organized and led by the young American, Brooke Dolan. Ironically it was a foreign member of this expedition, Ernst Schaefer, a young German naturalist, who accounted for the next giant panda. He shot a young female that was little more than a baby on the 13th May 1931 at Shen-wei in Wassuland. In addition Brooke Dolan and his companions acquired three adult specimens from the local inhabitants. One of these was donated to the Metropolitan Museum of Natural History at Nanking, while the other two together with Schaefer's infant giant panda were mounted in a fine family group set in naturalistic surroundings in the Free Natural History Museum at Philadelphia.

So far three westerners had killed one adult and one juvenile giant panda. Not every expedition that went to China to search for the animal, however, was rewarded with a personal success in this way. For instance, Floyd Tangier Smith, a colourful character who was later to play a major role in the pursuit of the live giant panda, apparently failed to qualify as the fourth panda slayer. He led the Marshall Field Zoological Expedition to South-east Asia from 1930 to 1932, at the same time that the Brooke Dolan expedition was in action, but as far as we know, Tangier Smith had to be content with providing his sponsors in Chicago with two more specimens secured through Chinese hunters to enhance the Roosevelt group already displayed there. As an official collector for this particular museum Tangier Smith became entrenched as a familiar landmark of panda country which few subsequent expeditions failed to miss. Meanwhile Jack Young, who, as we have

Ernst Schaefer with recently killed panda cub and tragopan

Family group of stuffed pandas in the Philadelphia Natural History Museum, collected by the Brooke Dolan expedition. (Right) Schaefer's infant panda as a mounted specimen in the Philadelphia Museum

already mentioned, played a supporting role in the Roosevelt expedition of 1928, shortly afterwards organized his own quest to the same regions and returned with two skins complete with skulls. One of these was donated to the Shanghai Museum and the other went to the American Museum of Natural History in New York. Claims have been made that both Floyd Tangier Smith and Jack Young actually shot giant pandas themselves, but there seems to be no conclusive evidence that this was, in fact, so.

The great American natural history institutions vied with one another to obtain giant pandas and once the ice had been broken with respect to panda-shooting priorities, the manner in which their specimens were obtained seemed less important than the numbers involved. The United States National Museum in Washington had found a reliable panda purveyor in Dr. David Crockett Graham, a missionary at the West China Union University. Although he apparently never spilled a drop of panda blood in his life, he took full advantage of his favourable on-the-spot position to purchase specimens from local hunters. Between the years 1929 and 1942 he provided Washington with no less than fifteen skins and skeletons.

Yet there was a certain prestige attached to a museum sponsoring its own collecting trip, and one expedition after another departed hastily for China, each with its sights set upon the giant panda. As a result, these hunting parties began to overlap with increasing frequency. In 1934, it was reported that Brooke Dolan and Ernst Schaefer were off once again, convinced that they now knew the vital secret of successful panda shooting. It was their belief that rather than look for the animal on the ground, where it

The West China Union University at Chengtu

was virtually invisible in the jungle of bamboo and rhododendron, the hunter should concentrate on scanning the trees. When asleep, or sunbathing in the fork of a tree, the giant panda was a comparatively conspicuous target. These underhand tactics do not seem to have stood them in good stead and their expedition faded into oblivion as far as the story of the panda killers is concerned.

It was yet another American expedition that chalked up the third giant panda to fall to western guns. In 1934 Dean Sage, accompanied by his wife Anne, T. Donald Carter and William G. Sheldon, departed for the highlands of Szechuan province in search of unusual game. The wild blue sheep or bharal was one of their goals and they managed to shoot four of these before the fogs of October defeated them. But as Sage wrote later: "There were other and more exciting game to wet our appetites, namely the giant panda. . . This rare and little known animal inhabits the dense bamboo jungles. . . To the best of our knowledge, only two giant pandas have ever been shot by white men. The spectacular appearance of this creature, his scarcity, and the extreme difficulty of hunting him on the rugged and treacherous bamboo-covered slopes; all these factors made him a prize for which we aspired with the keenest enthusiasm."

The party, therefore, made its way northward to panda territory and came to the valley of Cheng Wai, where it was rewarded with the first definite reports of the presence of the animal in the shape of two bei-shung skins discovered in a farmer's house. The quest was really on. Dean Sage described the dramatic events that followed: "Day after day we climbed the bamboo ridge of Cheng Wai and Mao Mo Gou, in the first of our optimism confident of

55

success, and as time went on less confident but ever hopeful." The months passed and although the expedition amassed a formidable collection of bird and mammal skins for the American Museum of Natural History, by December 1934, they had still failed to achieve their main objective. As Donald Carter expressed it, this was "to secure the animals and necessary accessories for a proposed giant panda group". It sounded prosaic enough when put in this way. Panda signs in the shape of chewed ends of bamboo and droppings were plentiful and the Americans even managed to buy a skin from a Chinese hunter, but their own endeavours yielded absolutely nothing. Yet the effort required was enormous. Dean Sage wrote: "It was hard work climbing the mountains, thrashing through snow and creeping over ice-covered ledges. We set spear traps; we searched acres and acres of bamboo-covered slopes with our field glasses, looking for a tell-tale white spot. We hunted with dogs. Unreliable curs that would run anything from a deer to a pheasant, they were a sore trial to our patience."

By early December the quest was virtually over. Mrs. Sage was

The valley of Mao Mo Gou where the Sage expedition hunted the giant panda. (Nat. Hist. Mag., N.Y.)

lame in her game knee and Donald Carter had gone on to Tsaopo, the first step of their homeward journey, to pack skins left there. Only one day's hunting remained, and Dean Sage and William Sheldon decided to make the most of it. They had in the meantime acquired a vicious dog which was reputedly ready to tackle anything and, it was hoped, fierce enough to hold and worry a giant panda. Encouraged by this and a panda trail discovered the previous day, they determined to make one final all-out effort. So the two Americans accompanied by four Chinese hunters and their dogs, including the new savage one, set out early on the morning of 8th December.

They combed the vertical planes of bamboo jungle and found a panda track that at first appeared to be only two to three days old. But by one o'clock the party was dispirited. The dogs showed little interest in the trail and it looked as though this their last excursion would be as fruitless as all the previous attempts. Since there seemed to be nothing to lose, the dogs were unleashed to range about for a while in the hope that they might pick up the scent. The rest of the hunters disappeared ahead of Dean Sage and his gun-bearer Wong. Sage climbed laboriously up on to a ledge and was resting disconsolately against a spruce tree when he noticed William Sheldon 50 yards above him. Suddenly the dogs gave tongue and he heard the unmistakable sound of crashing bamboo. Wong said the single word "Beishung!"

How did the leader of the expedition feel now that the moment of truth was imminent? This is the way Dean Sage recorded his emotions in his diary: "Up the ravine came the dogs, their barking growing steadily louder, and the bamboos crackling at a great rate. Suddenly, I heard the deep angry growl of a large animal, and I began to get really excited. And then—as if in a dream—I saw a giant panda coming through the bamboos about sixty yards away from me. He was heading straight up the ravine with the dogs at his heels. I fired but missed. The panda made a right angle turn and came straight for the ledge I was standing on. I fired again.

"He came right on, not running—walking rapidly is the only way to describe it. His head hung low and swayed from side to side. His tongue was out, and he was panting. He appeared to be looking at the ground and apparently did not see me at all. I frantically worked the bolt of my rifle and snapped the hammer on an empty chamber. In a daze thoughts flashed through my mind: 'No more bullets; what'll I do? He's only twenty feet away, now fifteen, he's coming straight at me. Can I kill him with the butt of my rifle?' I felt a cartridge thrust into my hand. Wong had seen

my predicament. . . I jammed it into my gun and fired it into the bei-shung's fur. He was less than ten feet from me! At the same moment Bill shot from above, and the animal, struck by our bullets, rolled over and over down the slope and came to stop against a tree fifty yards below.

"We had killed a giant panda."

Once again, as in the case of the Roosevelt brothers, two American hunters had killed a giant panda between them. Their jubilation after the event is also recorded in Dean Sage's diary: "It was, of course, absolutely fantastic and utterly incredible that I had seen and shot a Giant Panda, that almost fabulous animal. But I am forgetting the rest of the story. Bill came flying down the mountain in a frenzy. I had forgotten him completely! I found he had been shooting at the panda from above! We both practically had hysterics on the spot, and so did the men. We fired all the rest of our bullets in the air, jumped around like loons and scream-ed ourselves hoarse. It appeared now that Wong had fired two barrels of ball from my shotgun and so believed he had taken part in the killing, but we never found any evidence to confirm this. However, every one was delighted, so it did not matter much."

Before beginning the triumphal procession back to camp, the

Hunters triumphant. From left to right: Mrs. Sage, Dean Sage and William Sheldon

Giant panda group in the American Museum of Natural History. The specimen on the left is the one shot by the Sage expedition. (Photo: Amer. Mus. Nat. Hist.)

Americans examined the "most coveted trophy" that China had to offer the zoological world. The slaughtered panda, just under 5 feet in length and weighing about 225 pounds, proved to be an old female who looked as if she were a nursing mother. Within an hour-and-a-half the body had been skinned and her skeleton and viscera removed. Such as remained of her carcass was then abandoned. The vital portions of the animal's anatomy were taken back to the American Museum of Natural History and the expedition gloried in the fact that their mission was completed successfully. Not only had two members of the party achieved the honour of becoming joint third on the official list of western panda-slayers but, for the first time, scientists were provided with the opportunity to study the internal anatomy of the animal.

As we have seen, by the end of 1934 one European and four Americans had personally participated in the shooting of three giant pandas. Theodore and Kermit Roosevelt had accounted for one adult male, Ernst Schaefer, the German zoologist, for a baby, and Dean Sage and William Sheldon for an elderly nursing female. Then, in 1935, Britain entered the panda-killing race when Captain H. C. Brocklehurst shot one and according to some authorities two. He was a former game warden in the Sudan who undertook a solitary expedition to Wassuland and while there shot a fully grown adult male, so officially becoming the sixth Westerner to kill a giant panda. His specimen was duly mounted and caused a considerable sensation when displayed at the Big Game Exhibition held in Berlin in 1937.

Given the very great efforts involved, the total bag of giant pandas seems remarkably low. In fact, compared with the wholesale destruction of orang-utans and other rare animals that has occurred once the West began to take an interest in them, it seems almost insignificant. Even when we take into consideration the encouragement given to local Chinese hunters by the demands from panda-hungry museums, the black-and-white giant seems to have eluded its pursuers with remarkable success. Such giant panda victims as were claimed during the course of all this feverish activity did benefit zoology to some extent, for thanks to the expeditions of the late twenties and early thirties a little more was now known about the animal's distribution, habits and anatomy. But even though it could now be viewed in a state of suspended animation in many of the world's larger museums, the giant panda still remained an oriental enigma and perhaps the most tantalizing challenge presented to man by the whole of the animal kingdom.

the panda
pursued

CHAPTER FOUR

WHILE the trophy-hunters and explorers, apparently quite uninhibited by the rarity of the giant panda or the discomfort and difficulties of hunting in panda country, attempted to satisfy the clamorous demand for dead specimens from the museums of America and, to a lesser extent, Europe, more far-seeing and ambitious hunters nursed their dreams of capturing the coveted prize alive. Such a quest would be a gamble, a shot in the dark, but the impact that a real live black-and-white teddy bear would produce on the now panda-conscious West seemed, to two men at least, to justify the financial risk. Both were Americans, and their story and its sequel appear to spring straight from the pages of a Hollywood script.

The first of the two men we have already mentioned. He was the animal collector with the colourful name of Floyd Tangier Smith who had led the Marshall Field Expedition in 1930–2. Around about 1934 he was reported to be making urgent attempts to be the first to succeed with a live capture. A Shanghai resident, he had been a banker in the Orient, had then turned to big game hunting, and finally to collecting. By 1934 he was already in his early fifties and had acquired considerable knowledge of panda country. He knew the local inhabitants well and had organized them to assist him in his exploits. Despite this, he had so far failed.

While Tangier Smith's native hunters were combing the remote bamboo mountain forests, another American was laying plans in New York. In the summer of 1934, William Harvest Harkness, Jnr., was making preparations to provide the Bronx Zoo with a living panda. He had already caused a great stir by catching several live Komodo dragons for them—spectacular giant monitor lizards from small islands in the middle of the then Dutch East Indies—and delivering them safely in May of that year. In the early autumn, accompanied by four strapping young men in whose company, it was said, he resembled a terrier amongst a bevy of Great Danes, he set sail for the East again on an even more exciting quest.

The famous animal collector Tangier Smith

We know comparatively little about William Harkness except that he had some zoological qualifications and a long-standing yen for travel and adventure in faraway places. For over ten years he had swopped explorers' books, stories and schemes with a striking, dark-haired, New York dress designer who, in a frantic last-minute ceremony, became Mrs. Ruth Harkness just two short weeks before he departed on the panda trail. In order to avoid embarrassing incidents in an otherwise all-male expedition, the

Ruth Harkness. (From *The Lady and the Panda*)

bride was left behind in America, consoled only by the thought that perhaps one day she would be able to accompany her husband on a future trip. As it happened, she was destined to be disappointed.

After a series of lively and much-reported misadventures in the Celebes Sea and Borneo, the William Harkness expedition reached Shanghai late in January 1935. By this time, only two of the original party remained and, when his last companion was then recalled to New York, Harkness was left completely alone. During the months that followed, everything went wrong. Frustrations, delays and disasters mounted up until, in February 1936, Harkness lay dead in Shanghai, apparently never having set eyes on the elusive panda.

From various sources Ruth Harkness later pieced together as best she could the course of events during her husband's thirteen-month stay in China. It seems that he began by teaming up with a young Englishman who, like himself, had an urge to travel into remote corners of the world, and another man that she describes only by his nickname of "Zoology Jones". "Zoology", according to her, was an unsuccessful soldier-of-fortune in his fifties, who had hunted in panda country for nearly twenty years, and who had acquired several panda skins from native hunters, but had never encountered the living animal. Although Mrs. Harkness never once mentions the older's man's real name, it is almost certain that "Zoology Jones" is none other than Tangier Smith. Not only is he the right age, with the right background, but, as the Shanghai expert on pandas, he was the obvious person for the stranded Harkness to contact. Furthermore, the authors Willy Ley and Herbert Wendt both refer to an association between William Harkness and Tangier Smith at the time.

Before departing on the long boat journey up the Yangtze River, Harkness attempted to obtain formal authorization for the expedition from the Academia Sinica in Nanking, the branch of the Chinese Government that controlled all educational and scientific activities and from which foreign scientists had to acquire permits. This proved to be a lengthy procedure and eventually, impatient to be on their way, the three men set off without official blessing.

They reached Szechuan Province, on the very threshold of panda country, only to be turned back at Kiating by the Chinese authorities, who refused to allow foreigners to enter what was, at that time, "politically unstable" territory. As a result, they were forced to spend an uncomfortable summer in the intense heat of the bustling river-port of Chungking. With the arrival of autumn the three disappointed men decided to return to Shanghai to make yet another approach to the Chinese Government for official backing. Eventually, after still more delays, the long-awaited permission was forthcoming in the January of 1936. But, ironically, it came too late. William Harkness was by now a sick man and he died of some mysterious illness late in February, back in the city where he had begun his unhappy quest.

"Zoology Jones," alias Tangier Smith, had in the meantime, it seems, returned once again to panda country, and did not witness Harkness' death. Ruth Harkness writes: "'Zoology' had been up-country expecting Bill to join him at the time that Bill died. He continued the expedition half-heartedly for a time, and then finally left the funds that Bill had sent him with missionaries to pay his hunters to continue collecting." In the spring of 1936, he must have gone again to Shanghai, for it was there, in July, that he came face to face with his late partner's widow.

On recovering from the shock of her husband's death, Ruth Harkness, much to the surprise of her sophisticated friends, had left the United States in April to "inherit" the expedition. It was her avowed intention to complete his task and fulfil their dream of bringing home a live giant panda. She had no practical experience of animal collecting and one of her first acts on reaching Shanghai was to contact "Zoology Jones". He did not exactly welcome her with open arms and was as discouraging about her ideas as possible: "No foreign woman could travel alone in that country. There were bandits; there were petty officials to stop you on one pretext or another . . . dysentry . . . The sensible thing to do, apparently, was to join forces with Zoology, who planned to go up in the autumn on a collecting trip." For some reason, she resisted this offer, determined to go all out for just the panda, rather than become involved in gathering up a general collection of mammals and birds.

It is almost certain that this was not their only point of disagreement. A more serious rift appears to have developed between them. Probably it was the classic case of the experienced but disillusioned professional versus the enthusiastic novice; perhaps, too, there were financial complications. In her book *The Lady and the Panda*, written two years later, Ruth Harkness has little more to add about either "Zoology" or his projected expedition. As we shall see later, this omission was undoubtedly far from accidental.

Towards the end of August, after making little progress with her own plans, she was considerably heartened by a phone call from the famous American-born Chinese hunter, Jack Young. He was well known for his part in many scientific expeditions into Tibet and Western China, and had accompanied the Roosevelt brothers on their epic trip in 1928. Not only did he offer to help her in any way he could, but introduced her to his younger brother, Quentin, who was to become her invaluable right-hand-man in the weeks that followed.

Scarcely twenty years old, Quentin Young, a shy, tall, loose-limbed boy, was a crack-shot whose great goal in life was to shoot a giant panda for the Nanking Museum. He not only spoke good English, but also knew the Szechuanese dialect. Above all, he was not particularly concerned about financial rewards. Together Ruth Harkness and the Youngs quickly laid their plans and assembled the necessary equipment. Somewhere in Shanghai, tucked away

Quentin Young. (From *The Lady and the Panda*)

in a garage, they unearthed some of her husband's original stores, including a collection of outsize male clothing. Woollen underwear, trousers, an old tweed jacket and even a pair of gigantic masculine boots were miraculously whittled down by ingenious Chinese tailors and shoemakers to fit Mrs. Harkness' 5-foot 4-inch frame. All unwanted stores, including seven army saddles complete with blankets, halters and spurs, were auctioned to raise funds.

The American Embassy had advised her to apply to the Academia Sinica in Nanking for the usual permit, but after the delays and frustrations that her husband had encountered on a similar quest, she decided that she "did not propose to cool my heels waiting for government red tape to be unwound". On 26th September she and Quentin Young departed for the interior. After the tedium of the usual 1,500 mile Yangtze boat trip, they reached the disembarkation port of Chungking, there to be greeted by the news that a rival expedition for live pandas had passed through ahead of them nearly three weeks before. In her book, Ruth Harkness makes no mention of the members of this other expedition, although she must surely have known who they were. Reading between the lines, it seems highly likely that the rival group was led by "Zoology Jones", alias Tangier Smith. He had learned of her successful negotiations just over three weeks before her actual date of departure from Shanghai. He was already preparing for an autumn trip and was no doubt in a position to move rapidly, once his mind was made up. The thought that she, despised novice, might get to panda country first and beat him to the post as the first westerner to bring a live panda out of the interior, was probably too much for him. The fact that his native hunters had been out searching for some time meant that a valuable quarry might already have been located and was simply sitting waiting to be picked up. Worse still, the hunters had been paid by the local missionaries with funds left there by him, but belonging originally to William Harkness. The situation required immediate action.

With the two rival groups converging hopefully on panda country, it was a toss-up as to who was going to win the prize. For Ruth Harkness, the overland journey of more than 300 miles was a colourful and eventful one, involving absconding, opium-addicted, Chinese porters, and an unwelcome bodyguard of sixteen tenacious soldiers. At one point, following the loss of chair-coolies, they were forced to process with as much dignity as possible in wheelbarrows, but this was a luxury compared with the later stages of the trek, when they had to move on foot through the bamboo thickets in the mountains.

At Wenchuan, the last outpost before the panda wilds, Quentin Young tried with little success to obtain the assistance of local hunters and porters for the last gruelling lap of the expedition. "A certain Wang of the town came to him and offered his services. Wang, it seemed, was Zoology's hunter, and lived very nicely in the town without bothering himself much about going out to hunt. He informed Quentin that he knew that he was still being paid each month from money that had been sent to Zoology by the foreign devil's husband before he died, but that made no difference—for still more he would work for us . . . we decided that as

Ruth Harkness on her way to panda country. (From The Lady and the Panda*)*

long as we had secured porters we would continue the next morning and trust to luck to find honest and efficient hunters up in the mountains."

However, just before they departed from Wenchuan, their breakfast in the Buddhist Ghost Temple was interrupted by an ancient, leather-faced, toothless and squint-eyed little man accompanied by two mongrel dogs be-decked with tinkling bells. His name was Lao Tsang and he claimed to be a great hunter and an influential headsman of his district. As he insisted that he knew where pandas could be found and that he could lead the party there, they hired him on the spot and, with two porters, moved off westwards. After a few days of rough climbing, Mrs. Harkness was beginning to lose heart. "Nearing the top of the ridge in the late afternoon, when I was tired enough to have burst into tears, we suddenly came on Panda sign. Pure gold couldn't have been more exciting. Carefully Yang stowed away the droppings and on we went." But this first clue proved to be disappointing. When examined by Quentin, it was pronounced to be too old to indicate the definite presence of a giant panda.

They broke camp the following morning and made for the village of Tsaopo, in the ancient Kingdom of Wassu. There Quentin interviewed native hunters who came to offer their services and the following morning he went off exploring for three days, leaving Ruth Harkness behind. He returned with encouraging reports about the neighbouring country and by 4th November the expedition's first panda camp was established, one day's march from the village. In anticipation of the ferocious quarry they were about to encounter, Quentin Young had sent back for extra wire and ropes for the traps, a collar and chain, a big pair of iron tongs to hold the panda down with, and a fine red cock to sacrifice to the god of the mountain to ensure good hunting.

Mrs. Harkness stayed at the base camp and prepared to settle down for a month or six weeks, while Quentin established a camp for himself higher in the mountains and a third scout camp. Within a few days Quentin was back, firing his gun in high spirits. Everything was going splendidly and Mrs. Harkness was to join him at his camp the next day. Climbing through the moist landscape, past bamboo thickets, patches of snow, and giant rhododendrons 30 to 40 feet tall, she reached Camp Two soaked to the skin on the evening of 8th November. The following day she was to make history.

In the morning they set off—Mrs. Harkness, Quentin Young, old Lao Tsang and the local hunters—to inspect the traps. At the first one she saw "A bent sapling with a wire noose in a tiny pitfall just big enough for an animal's foot. The leafy covering would give way under the weight, releasing a cleverly placed peg that held the noose; the sapling would spring up—and right then and there I had visions of an unwary Panda at our mercy." But the going was tough and the bamboo thickets were dripping wet and slimy. After a while Mrs. Harkness was "proceeding mostly on hands and knees, and only Yang remained behind to give me an occasional lift by the seat of my pants. Without warning, a shout went up from the jungle ahead of us. I heard Lao Tsang yell, the report of his blunderbuss musket, and then Quentin's voice raised in rapid and imperious Chinese. Falling, stumbling, or being dragged by Yang, we crashed through the bamboo."

Lao Tsang, it seemed, had seen a fully grown panda and shot at it. He and the other hunters has then rushed off after it. This made Ruth Harkness angry, as she had given strict instructions that there was to be no panda-killing while she was there (although she knew that Quentin Young was going to stay on and hunt them after she had left). On this occasion, Quentin did not join the chase, but stayed behind with Mrs. Harkness. "We listened for a moment, and went on a few yards farther where the bamboo

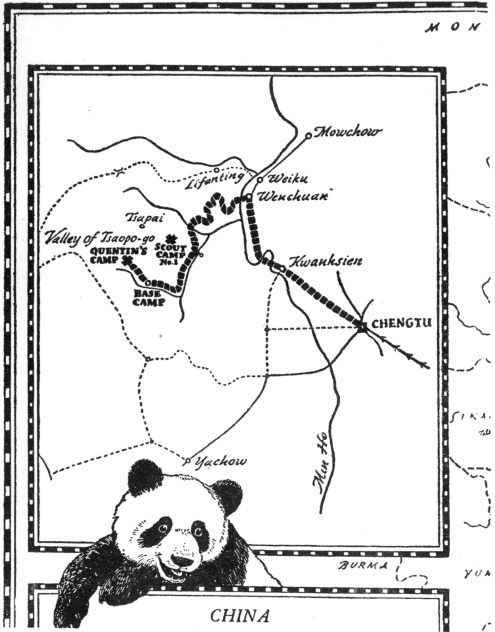

The map of the Ruth Harkness expedition

thinned slightly, giving way to a few big trees. Quentin stopped so short that I almost fell over him. He listened intently for a split second, and then went ploughing on so rapidly I couldn't keep up with him. Dimly through the waving wet branches I saw him near a huge rotting tree. I stumbled on blindly, brushing the water from my face and eyes. Then I too stopped, frozen in my tracks. From the old dead tree came a baby's whimper. I must have been momentarily paralysed, for I didn't move until Quentin came toward me and held out his arms. There in the palms of his two hands was a squirming baby *Bei-shung*."

This tiny creature, with its eyes still closed, was destined to become the first giant panda ever seen alive by the western world. In a few short months it was to become the most famous animal of the twentieth century. As Mrs. Harkness held it in her arms for the first time, she records simply that, "That little black-and-white ball nuzzled my jacket, and suddenly, with the sureness of age-old instinct, went straight to my breast."

There then began a frantic dash back to the base camp, where milk and nursing bottles were packed away. Quentin carried the baby panda tucked in between his inner and outer shirt as they slithered down the steep mountain slopes. At the camp all went well and they celebrated while the baby fed from its bottle. The animal weighed less than 3 pounds and was thought to be no more

Ruth Harkness nursing the baby panda, Su-Lin. (From The Lady and the Panda)

than ten days old. Ruth Harkness named it after Jack Young's wife, Su-Lin, whose name was best translated as "a little bit of something very cute". (Although it was found, on post-mortem, to be a male, throughout its short life the animal was thought to be a female.)

Great care was taken to supply the young panda with a snug cradle, their shirts, sweaters and towels being torn up to provide the necessary bedding. During these parental duties, porters arrived, bedraggled and weary, carrying heavy tongs, a stout collar, chains and padlocks, and a large red, sacrificial cock. Their comments on seeing the exact size of the captive panda are not recorded. Out of courtesy, a sacrificial ceremony was arranged and, by the light of flares, the unfortunate cockerel was stabbed through the neck three times, paper money was burned, wine poured on the earth, and fire-crackers let off. As an impromptu embellishment to the ceremony, Mrs. Harkness fired a revolver three times into the air.

She was now faced with the problem of getting Su-Lin back to the United States. Quentin accompanied her back to Chengtu and then returned to his promised reward of panda hunting in the hills. (In fact he not only killed one for the Nanking Museum, but a second one as well.) Su-Lin was proving an exhausting infant in more ways than one. Not only was there the problem of round-the-clock feeding, but also the perpetual bombardment of queries from the curious and fascinated Chinese. At Chengtu special arrangements were made for the panda to travel to Shanghai by air. After the overland journey from the mountains this was a great luxury and Mrs. Harkness could at last relax, if only momentarily. As she flew east to the coast, taking "a little bit of something very cute" with her, she was leaving behind her, under the gnarled roots of a great rhododendron tree in the mountains, the high price she had paid for it: a small sealed cardboard box containing her husband's ashes, that she had carried with her all the way in a steel cash-box to the panda country that he never saw.

At Shanghai airport the little woven bamboo basket containing Su-Lin was rushed to a waiting car to avoid the crowd of newspaper photographers and reporters, alerted by their agents in Chengtu. There followed days of chaos and confusion during which attempts were made to obtain permission to export the panda to America. The earliest boat was the *Empress of Russia* sailing on 27th November. Passages were booked and all went well until the very last minute. Then, after boarding the tender to go out to the ship, she was stopped by customs officials and brought

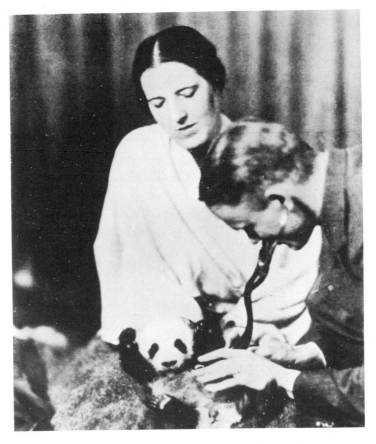

On arrival in Shanghai, Su-Lin receives a medical examination. (From *The Lady and the Panda*)

back. She had obtained no export permit and had paid no export tax. While the *Empress of Russia* sailed, she slept with Su-Lin on a bench in the Shanghai customs sheds. The following day was a nightmare of officialdom and panda husbandry mixed together, and the classic panda pun was printed in a newspaper for the first of many times: "Panda-monium in Shanghai Customs House".

Garbled newspaper reports of the situation began to appear, including wild guesses at the value of the panda. One report estimated the figure at 25,000 dollars, which did nothing to ease the export situation. Influential Americans in Shanghai rallied round, however, and on 2nd December the now voiceless Ruth Harkness and the baby panda sailed at last for the United States on the *President McKinley*, complete with an export tax receipt, an export permit and an animal passage voucher reading "One Dog, $20.00". The panda epoch was about to begin.

During her five crowded months in China, Ruth Harkness had not only achieved her goal and completed the work her husband began, but she had also pipped at the post the professional animal collector "Zoology Jones", alias Tangier Smith. In her book *The*

Lady and the Panda, she makes no mention of his activities or movements after she has acquired her panda. All we hear is that one of his native hunters (Wang) at Wenchuan tried to incite the soldiers in the town to prevent her from leaving with Su-Lin. Beyond this, nothing.

How is one to interpret this? What exactly was going on in the rival camp? Was the other expedition hot on the panda trail, or did Smith-Jones simply fade from the picture, as Mrs. Harkness would have us believe? There are some scattered clues that throw a strange, if somewhat multi-coloured light on the affair. They differ in certain vital respects, but nearly all agree on one intriguing point, namely that Mrs. Harkness was not, after all, the only successful panda captor in 1936. According to several reports, she was not even the first, that honour belonging in fact to Floyd Tangier Smith.

The only way to assess the validity of these statements is to examine them in turn. Taking the wildest one first, Herbert Wendt in *Out of Noah's Ark* claims that, far from being a dismal failure, the original William Harkness–Tangier Smith expedition succeeded in catching a young giant panda in 1936. They are supposed to have ear-marked it for the London Zoo, but "It breathed its last in Singapore. And William Harkness died about the same time in Shanghai." This seems highly improbable, as Harkness died in February and the expedition had more or less petered out towards the end of 1935.

In *Dragons in Amber*, Willy Ley makes a similar statement, but gives all the credit for the first panda capture to Tangier Smith: "Floyd T. Smith seemed to be the first to succeed. In 1936 he captured a giant panda which was destined for the London Zoological Garden. But the specimen died in Singapore." With no mention of William Harkness, this report could refer to any point in 1936 and could easily relate to a later expedition made by Tangier Smith alone. It could, in fact, relate to the mysterious "rival expedition" that was three weeks ahead of Ruth Harkness at Chengtu, on the way to the mountains. If Tangier Smith had been successful on that trip and hustled a living panda hurriedly back to the coast, he might well have done so with some degree of secrecy, if only because his hunters were still being financed with William Harkness funds, thus giving Ruth some claim to the spoils. This could also have been the reason for the animal being sent off to London, rather than New York, his original zoo contact in the West.

The plot thickens with a newspaper report from Singapore in

which secrecy features again. S. H. Benson, writing in the *Scottish Field* in 1942 recalls that "about 1936" a friend in Singapore sent him a cutting from a Singapore paper in which banner headlines declared that two pandas had been caught for the London Zoo by Tangier Smith. The article reads: "Asia's rarest animal, a giant panda, on its way to London Zoo, died between Hong Kong and Shanghai on the French Liner *Andre Lebon*. Only the third animal of its type to be caught alive, it joined the vessel at Shanghai. The heavier of the two caught, which weighed 200 lb., died, but the other weighing about 100 lb., and carefully dyed to appear like a brown bear in order not to attract attention, was safely taken to Shanghai. . ."

If we are to believe this report, the unhappy Tangier Smith must have made a desperate attempt to beat Ruth Harkness to it by the ingenious method of disguising his animal as a young bear and thus getting it through the customs without official delays. If the date, 1936, is accepted, then he must almost certainly have won the race, as regards being the first person to take a living panda out of China, as she did not finally get away until December. (Weigold was, of course, the first occidental to hold a living giant panda, but his short-lived encounter seems to have been over-looked in all accounts of "who was first".) The situation in Shanghai, with the two successful panda-hunters, both jealously guarding their prizes and frantically trying to board ship for the West, must have been bizarre enough, but the ultimate confusion that would have arisen if Tangier Smith's brown-stained protégé had survived the voyage to England is even more intriguing to contemplate. Presumably both the New York and the London Zoo would have been offered the "very first" giant panda ever to leave the Orient. If only this had happened, a great deal would undoubtedly have been forced into the open and we would now be able to tell the whole story in much more detail.

An interesting point in the Singapore statement is that the dyed panda was the third to have been taken alive. As the original Weigold panda was so little known, this indicates that Su-Lin, as well as Tangier Smith's bigger one, had already been caught and implies that Ruth Harkness was at least first with the capture itself. If we believe a report in the *China Journal* by Arthur Sowerby she was also first to export a panda, despite the rumours of Tangier Smith's 1936 success. He states that "Mr Smith . . . with the help of his native hunters, succeeded in the spring of 1937 in securing two adult giant pandas, one a fully adult male weighing, it was said, about 400 lbs., the other, an adult female, weighing about 200 lbs. Of these the male died at Chungking on the Upper Yangtze from blood-poisoning through an injury to its foot when it was trapped. The other died on the voyage from Shanghai to London before it reached Singapore, presumably from the excessive heat of the Tropics."

This report tallies in most ways with the previous one, except for the date and the weight of the animals. If Sowerby is correct, then Mrs. Harkness was already safely in America some months before Tangier Smith reaped his short-lived reward. Unfortunately Sowerby's writings show considerable bias in Ruth Harkness' favour and, like her book, reduce to a minimum any mention of Tangier Smith's activities, so that they are not entirely above suspicion.

Whatever the exact dates were, it seems certain that Tangier Smith did capture two pandas at some point before the summer of 1937. Or was it three? Let him speak for himself. Later in 1937 he came to England and broadcast on the B.B.C. on this topic. His comments were as follows:

"It has been my great good fortune to have been the active agent in effecting the capture of the only three giant pandas that have ever been taken alive. That has been possible only after some several years of careful study of the animal's habits and the systematic organization of the inhabitants in a certain area. My central collecting headquarters are at a village called Chaopo. . . The first specimen thus secured—the baby panda recently sold to Chicago —it was not my privilege to take home myself. It had been brought into Chaopo at a time when I was absent some several days before a party of travellers pitched their camp about fifteen miles up the valley from Chaopo, and it was sold to them for a tempting cash price. There were more than forty other animals and birds collected in the camp at the same time, but nothing but the panda was purchased by the visitors, and I brought most of the others with me on this trip to England. . . . I have not yet finished with the business of capturing pandas. I expect to return to China in the very near future, and when I do it will be to go all out for bigger and better pandas."

Alongside this statement, the other discrepancies fade into insignificance. We are now dealing with a major falsification. But whose? Was Ruth Harkness lying when she wrote her account of the dramatic capture of Su-Lin? Had she, in reality, bought it knowingly from Tangier Smith's collecting centre and then fled for the coast? Or was Tangier Smith lying, trying to distort the whole situation to save his professional face?

Su-Lin was weighed as often as possible

Most certainly, the baby panda that Tangier Smith refers to was Su-Lin, Chicago being that animal's ultimate destination as we shall see in the next chapter. Also Ruth Harkness' village of Tsaopo was without doubt Tangier Smith's village of Chaopo (the difference being merely one of spelling, not pronunciation). The mystery, therefore, surrounds the action that took place at that spot in the autumn of 1936. Re-reading the Harkness account, there are several strange features that make one wonder. When so many experts had trailed the panda without success, it was very odd that, within days, a complete novice could find a young one. Tangier Smith, on the other hand, had had hunters out working for months, if not years, and if anyone was likely to have located one, it was he. According to another report altogether, Tangier

Smith had "had his eye on Su-Lin for a long time and had just waited for her to grow a little older". As the animal's eyes were still shut and it only weighed 2 or 3 pounds, the "long time" he had been watching it could not have been so very long.

What can one possibly conclude from all this? Was Ruth Harkness a courageous, dedicated widow desperately completing her late husband's unfinished business, or an imaginative, scheming liar? Was Tangier Smith an honest, victimized professional, or was he a neurotic, embittered man, deliberately falsifying the evidence to save his pride? Perhaps there is yet another answer. Perhaps they were both innocent, but were thrown into conflict by the dishonesty of certain of their companions. Quentin Young and his hunters, for example, had ample opportunity to buy the information concerning Su-Lin's whereabouts from Tangier Smith's hired men. They could even have bought the animal itself and "planted" it in the old dead tree. Alternatively Tangier Smith's Wenchuan hunter, Wang, could have lied to his employer, inventing the story of Su-Lin's sale to cover his shame at allowing newcomers to find the panda so near to his supposedly well-watched territory.

Unless some new evidence comes to light, we shall never know the true story. All we can be sure of is that a baby panda was brought out of the Orient just before Christmas 1936 and that it caught the imagination of the whole western world. But the cost was high. Already it had claimed the life of William Harkness, turned two remarkable explorers against one another, and forced someone into uttering deliberate and serious falsehoods. But these problems and quarrels must now be allowed to fade into the mists of the cold mountain forests of Szechuan, for aboard the *President McKinley* a Very Important Panda was rapidly approaching America. Su-Lin was about to arrive at San Francisco.

pandas in America

pandas in America

CHAPTER FIVE

Su-Lin installed at Brookfield Zoo, Chicago. (From Waring and Wells)

ON 18TH DECEMBER 1936, the Western World encountered for the very first time a living giant panda. For Ruth Harkness the experience was even more exhausting and chaotic than the departure from China; "The final consensus of the press was that not since Bernard Shaw had a foreign celebrity received such a reception as Su-Lin." Droves of reporters and newspaper photographers jostled for position. Flash bulbs exploded and people shouted. Officialdom argued and worried. For a human star this is all sweet music, but for a very young animal—and Su-Lin's first milk tooth was only just breaking through as they docked in San Francisco—it can be disastrous. Ruth Harkness had to be constantly on her guard. It was as much as she could do to stop the animal being cuddled literally to death, so strong was its appeal to pent-up maternal urges.

One of the biggest problems was caused by the fact that, like Bernard Shaw, Su-Lin was a carnivore turned vegetarian. Although still subsisting entirely on baby food, the time would come when bamboo shoots would be the order of the day and Mrs. Harkness had very wisely collected and brought with her some specimens of these plants from the mountains of Szechuan. It was her intention to present them to botanical experts for examination, so that the best substitute for them could be found before Su-Lin reached bamboo-munching age. Unfortunately, the United States Department of Agriculture officials had other ideas. Finally, after a great deal of controversy, it was agreed that the vital plants could be allowed into the country providing that every speck of dirt was first washed from their roots.

After various mishaps in San Francisco and considerable argument as to which airline was going to have the honour of conveying the animal across the States, Su-Lin and owner eventually managed to board an east-bound train after a wild taxi dash across the city. Two days later the whole circus was repeated in Chicago, but this time zoological experts were present in the shape of zoo director Edward Bean and his son Robert, then curator of mammals. They tried to persuade Mrs. Harkness to leave Su-Lin with them, but this only set off a new type of argument. Ruth Harkness refused to sell the animal, insisting that she would only part with it in exchange for backing for another expedition. She apparently had a horror of being called a commercial animal dealer and drew a subtle but, to her, all-important distinction between the two kinds of payment. More cynical observers pointed out that the only real difference was that backing an expedition would cost more.

Leaving a disappointed Robert Bean at the Chicago Zoo, Su-Lin journeyed on to New York and another battery of flash bulbs. Here the confusion and tension became greater still, and it began to tell on the panda itself. Su-Lin became constipated and it was obvious that the animal needed to be in expert hands. The expert hands themselves were not so sure, however. Much to Mrs. Harkness' disgust, the zoo officials in New York approached the subject of the panda's acquisition with some caution. After days of public acclaim and adulation, their guarded, critical attitude came as a severe shock. Why, they wanted to know, were its back legs so much weaker than its front ones? One group of visiting officials pronounced that it must have rickets. Doubts were expressed about how long the little creature would live, after all it had been through. Then there was the question of feeding it, the difficulties of obtaining supplies of the correct bamboo, and the dangers of using diet substitutes.

The panda story inspires the world of commercial advertising

Later, Ruth Harkness wrote of her exasperation and depression: "Wherever authorities had written about rare animals, you felt that every zoological society of any note whatever was sighing for a Panda, that life would not be complete until they had one" . . . but . . . "All seemed afraid of the risk involved in raising such a small specimen to healthy adulthood. And no one of them wanted to back me for another expedition; they offered me only a fraction of what my first one had cost. Time went on, and I became more and more discouraged . . . The whole business looked as though it were going to end in utter failure . . . Was I a little insane, or had I just imagined that bringing a live Panda to America was worth anything to this great rich country of ours? When I had sunk to the lowest point of discouragement, the only thing I could think of that I wanted to do was to pack everything up, take Su-Lin and go back to the border of Tibet. And perhaps if I'd had sufficient money, I would have done just that." Luckily for the American public, she was running short of funds and had to stay put.

By now Su-Lin had taken on the role of a panda ambassador and was virtually changing the whole attitude of western civilization towards the species. Clearly it was unthinkable to invade the homeland of such a charming creature and gun it down as a trophy or a museum specimen. A major conversion was achieved as a result of a visit from the original panda-killers, Theodore and Kermit Roosevelt. Su-Lin won them over in a few minutes. When Theodore, sitting on the floor of Ruth Harkness' apartment, with the small animal cradled in his arms, was asked whether he would like to see it eventually mounted and added to his panda group in the Chicago Field Museum, he retorted that "I'd as soon think of mounting my own son as I would this baby."

The Roosevelts were followed by other famous panda hunters, paying homage at Su-Lin's court. Brooke Dolan of the Philadelphia Academy of Natural Sciences paid a visit, as did Dean Sage and his wife. Like the others, Sage became an immediate convert declaring: "Mrs. Harkness, I'd never be able to shoot another Panda."

At about this time Ruth Harkness was honoured by the New York Explorer's Club. A staunchly masculine organization, it made the first exception to its all-male rule in inviting her to be guest of honour at its 33rd annual banquet. The dinner was held at the Plaza Hotel and Su-Lin was provided with a complete suite where all the windows could be thrown open to counteract the fierce blast of New York central heating. When the meal was over, the diminutive panda was carried ceremonially into the dining hall and

Su-Lin poses with her life story. (Chicago Zool. Soc.)

on to the speaker's platform where, to the delight of the 500 gentlemen explorers, it performed the ritual of broadcasting a few disgruntled bleats to the waiting American nation.

Despite the more ludicrous aspects of this and other such occasions, it is true to say that the growth of the panda cult surrounding Su-Lin added a very important nail to the coffin of the "huntin' and shootin' epoch". True, it still goes on today wherever the preferred quarry (other men) is not available. But, like war, it has lost a great deal of its glamour. Su-Lin was perhaps becoming not so much a Hairy Shirley Temple as a Furry Billy Graham.

For Ruth Harkness, however, the dilemma of what to do with a growing panda remained. In the end, fed up with the attitude of zoo officials in New York, she offered the animal to Chicago as a guest. They accepted with pleasure and Su-Lin was soon installed in the first-aid station of Brookfield Zoo, being looked after day and night by Robert Bean and his sister Mary.

The move to Chicago took place on 8th February 1937, making this the earliest date on which any zoo had housed a living giant panda. In a Chicago hotel room that night Mrs. Ruth Harkness awoke at midnight to give Su-Lin the usual nightly feed, remembered sleepily that after three months of turmoil she was at last alone, and returned weeping to her bed.

Two months later, in April, the Brookfield Zoo purchased Su-Lin, or, rather, "contributed" to Mrs. Harkness' next expedition. Although she had only just recovered from the strain of the first ordeal, she was already preparing to repeat the whole process in order to acquire a mate for Su-Lin. Unfortunately she, and everyone else, still held the view that Su-Lin was a female. There was no doubt in their minds. As we have already mentioned, the post mortem eventually revealed that they had all been mistaken and she was, in fact, a he. With her newly acquired expedition funds in her bag Mrs. Harkness was therefore sallying forth to secure a young male panda as a mate for a young male panda. (Although she was the first to make this mistake she was by no means the last, as we shall see later.)

With Su-Lin steadily putting on weight at a rate of 5 pounds a month and continuing to make friends and influence people, Ruth Harkness made her return journey to the bamboo forests in the Szechuan mountains. There, in Wassu country again, she trekked and trailed for three long months in search of a male panda. She found two live cubs, but to her great disappointment they both turned out to be females. One of them, named Diana, she brought successfully back to Chicago where she was able to introduce it to Su-Lin.

Although Diana had been caught in 1937, this panda did not reach Chicago Zoo until 18th February 1938. Su-Lin's weight in the meantime had shot up from 14 pounds to over 100 pounds, and when the two were put together the pioneer panda dwarfed the new arrival. Eventually, it was hoped, they would settle down quietly together, as Diana gradually caught up with the bulky Su-Lin. But unhappily in six short weeks Su-Lin was dead. The post mortem revealed that a piece of wood had become lodged in

Ruth Harkness introduces Diana (foreground) to the now much larger Su-Lin at Brookfield Zoo

the animal's throat. The cause of death was not a hopeless, inevitably lethal disease, just a freak accident. As if this were not bad enough, the zoo officials also learned from the dissection that, instead of two females, they had had a potential breeding pair. But on this score at least they need not have worried for, when Diana herself eventually succumbed on 3rd August 1942, she too proved to be a he.

Before this second sex-error was discovered, however, Mrs. Harkness was already off to the mountains again to find a young male panda as a mate for the now solitary Diana, commissioned to do so once more by the Chicago Zoo authorities. She left in the spring of 1938 and arrived at Chengtu at the beginning of June. A newspaper report from there a week later stated that she was about "to take possession of a 40-pound female panda cub captured for her by Quentin Young, a youthful Chinese-American. Young is reported to have a male panda staked, out in the hills." Ironically, it then adds: "With females in the majority, gentleman pandas are now in the heaviest demand."

Everything appeared to be set fair for Mrs. Harkness to achieve her hat-trick, but for some reason the project misfired. Presumably Young's new finds were poor specimens and died before they could be brought out of China. We can find no record of what happened to them. All we know is that by February 1939 Mrs. Harkness was in London, probably on her way back to the United States.

Despite her failure on this occasion, the Chicago Zoo did manage to obtain a third specimen, and did so in a rather unusual way. In the summer of 1938 a correspondent of the Chicago *Daily News*, A. T. Steele, made a wild claim that giant pandas were now a glut on the market. From Chengtu he sent his paper a photograph of four pandas sitting on a lawn. He also wrote an article with the heading PANDAS RARE? SOMEONE WAS REALLY KIDDING. As a piece of journalism it certainly struck a new note. When readers are bombarded day after day with the rarity and value of something, a startling and provocative reporting device that is sometimes used is to slant a story completely in the opposite direction. The trick is that there must be *some* facts to support the sudden twist. A photograph of four pandas on a lawn is just enough to trigger off the great switch. On the basis of the previously stressed rarity, four is a crowd. The shock story is under way. From then on it is a case of dragging in every panda going and a few that are only rumoured to be going. With some strong phrasing to help the tale along, the readers, relieved to find

Diana, now re-christened Mei-Mei, settles down to life in Chicago. (Chicago Zool. Soc.)

a crack at last in the star image, will soon be convinced. Here are some of the things that Steele claimed:

"Unless all signs fail, the United States is about to be glutted with giant pandas. Ever since word got around that the fancy prices paid in Chicago were offered elsewhere for captive pandas, West China has been panda-conscious. The result is that more pandas, dead and alive, are brought to Chengtu than one can shake a stick at . . . Panda pelts are a drug on the market. Yesterday I was offered four, at 8 American dollars apiece, with skulls thrown in. Pandas are not rare. It was not until Mrs. William Harkness came out here a couple of years ago that the mountain dwellers realized that the critters were of any use to anybody, and that they could get more fun and profit from chasing pandas than from collecting herbs or bamboo. Colorful tales have been woven for the American public about the supposed perils of panda hunting in Szechuan. As a matter of fact, the trip into the heart of the panda country from here is no more dangerous or difficult than a journey to the depths of the Wisconsin woods. The panda region . . . can be reached in two days by bus and horse—if one is in a hurry."

Steele goes on to explain that visitors no longer bother to hunt the pandas, they simply buy them from the locals. "The buyer getting to the hunter first with the fattest bank roll gets the panda. Giant panda prices, f.o.b. (freight on board) Chengtu, range between 25 and 180 dollars per head, although the latter is regarded locally as fabulously high."

This shattering information naturally met with more than just a surprised whistle at the offices of the Brookfield Zoo, Chicago. They had paid out hefty sums for their two pandas, enough at least to finance two expeditions to China, and they were not unreasonably annoyed at the suggestion that they had been duped. They immediately contacted the editor of the *Daily News*, Colonel Knox, and threw down the gauntlet. If pandas were so cheap and plentiful, they argued, he would presumably be quite prepared to present them with a third one for the Chicago Zoo. He agreed and straight away cabled Steele in Chengtu, instructing him to secure a giant panda and despatch it without delay to Chicago.

The interesting fact that emerges from this incident is that, although Steel had exaggerated wildly when he used words like "glut" and "drug on the market", his anti-rare, anti-exotic theme was not without some foundation. This was proved by the fact that, although he could not produce a panda by return of post, he did contrive to do so eventually. The archives show that it was 17

months and 8 days after his inflammatory article that he finally managed to complete the Chicago hat-trick that Ruth Harkness had been unable to achieve.

This third panda's name was Mei-Lan, meaning "pretty flower". Again it was a rather unsuitable title, for like the other two, Mei-Lan was ultimately proved to be a male. As a two-month old cub it had been carried 150 miles to Chengtu by a native hunter. Once there it had spent seven months in the grounds of the West China Union University. During that time four other pandas were brought in, but only Mei-Lan and one other survived. Although it is not possible to give an accurate date of birth, it seems likely that Mei-Lan was born towards the end of 1938. It was caught early in 1939, spent the summer in Chengtu and was flown out to Hong Kong in the autumn in the care of American photographer Roy Scott. From there it sailed for San Francisco on the *President Cleveland* arriving early in November. On the way to Chicago it stopped off for a four-day visit in Hollywood where its star status was carefully enhanced by an encounter with Dorothy

Mei-Lan as an adult at the Chicago Zoo. (Chicago Zool. Soc.)

Lamour and a garden party on the lawn of the Hotel Ambassador.

On 16th November it finally reached its new home, was greeted at the station by a fanfare from the Chinese Boy Scout drum corps, and met the resident panda Diana, now re-christened Mei-Mei. Mei-Lan, being nearly a year old at this point weighed about 80 pounds, but once again the newcomer was dwarfed by the resident, Mei-Mei now tipping the scales at 250 pounds.

From the beginning Mei-Lan was a sturdy, tough specimen, and went on to break all panda records for longevity in captivity, living contentedly at Brookfield throughout World War II and on into the fifties. The exact date of death was 5th September 1953, giving a zoo life of 13 years and 10 months and a total life span of nearly 15 years. At the time of writing we know of no other panda that has topped these figures.

For their pioneer role in the panda story the Brookfield Zoo, Chicago, deserves the highest praise. It is easy to smile at their errors over the sexes of the pandas, easy, that is, for anyone who has not actually attempted to sex one. The external differences between the male and female are so subtle that, even today, errors are still being made by skilled anatomists when faced with the living animal. Had it not been for the foresight of the Chicago officials, Sun-Lin might well have died in New York and such an event could easily have frightened off the zoo world and prevented them from making efforts to obtain further specimens. A great deal of our present-day knowledge of—and respect for—the giant panda would be lacking if this had been so.

New York's part in this story is harder to understand. It was for them that William Harkness had successfully acquired Komodo dragons and for them that he had set out again for panda country. It is rather surprising then that they did not snap up Su-Lin for their collection at the Bronx Zoo. Whatever their reasons, there can be little doubt that they were rather crestfallen when Chicago's gamble succeeded so brilliantly, for after a while they started negotiating with China to see what could be done for panda-less New York. It was probably the arrival of Chicago's second panda Diana/Mei-Mei that really roused them to action because we know that it was only a matter of a week or two after this that they began to tackle the problem in earnest.

The initiator of the scheme that was to bring them their first captive specimen was Dean Sage, a trustee of the New York Zoological Society. In March 1938 he suggested to Edward Cunningham of the University faculty that it would be mutually beneficial to the University of New York and to the West China Union University at Chengtu if it could be arranged for these two institutions to "join forces in a co-operative educational venture". Chengtu, he argued, "was situated at the very edge of one of the richest areas for the collection of scientific material of all sorts in the whole world. They also had a trained staff capable of making collections. In addition, there was the valuable factor of their close and friendly relationship with the central government, which would enable them to export materials collected. All this work could be done by them at low cost and the fruits of a rich and hitherto unexploited field could be made available to scientific institutions in this country, which had neither the financial means nor the political influence necessary for sending out expensive expeditions . . .".

In return, New York would aid Chengtu with "educational and scientific material such as films, technical journals, lantern slides, current scientific books, scientific instruments etc.", and the general development of their scientific department.

To the idealists this sounded like an inspired plan for improving international goodwill and education. To the cynics it sounded like a clever scheme for acquiring a cheap panda. When he wrote off to Chengtu University, Dean Sage admits that "In my letter I did not forget to mention that the one thing I wanted first of all was a live giant panda cub, if possible a pair of cubs, male and female." He goes on to say that "It had been, ever since my return from China, my desire to obtain one of these animals for the Zoological Society, and although efforts on my part had thus far been unavailing, I felt that here at last was the opportunity that would materialize." We could perhaps feel a little more sympathy for him in his earlier difficulties, were it not for the fact that fifteen months earlier he had sat in Ruth Harkness' New York apartment playing with Su-Lin at a time when she was desperately trying to find a good home for the little animal.

Be that as it may, the Chengtu authorities welcomed the exchange scheme and immediately sent word out to the native hunters in the hills. Frank Dickinson, a missionary at the West China Union University was in charge of the project, but it was his wife who made the vital contact. She was on a sketching trip at Kwanhsien, a village about sixty miles from Chengtu, when she was approached at her work by a Chinese woman who told her that a baby panda had been caught somewhere further west and was being brought into the village. Mrs. Dickinson went into action, the hunter was soon found, and before long the young panda was playing quietly in the Dickinson's home at the University. During its three weeks as the Dickinson family pet it acquired the nickname of Pandora. Dr. Roy C. Spooner, a colleague of Frank Dickinson's, was due for home leave and agreed to accompany the animal to the United States. They flew to Hong Kong in a small four-seater China National Airways plane, leaving Chengtu on 18th May 1938, but not before a last-minute panic about clearance papers. These were finally obtained from the Commissioner of Education—sitting on his veranda still wearing his dressing gown—at 6 a.m. on the actual morning of the flight. Pandora sailed for America on the *President Cleveland* (the same ship that, the following year, was to transport Mei-Lan to the United States), arriving at San Francisco 9th June, where she was met by Dean Sage himself. Sage rushed her on to a plane and had her safely in New York by the following afternoon.

And so, on 10th June 1938, New York was able to join Chicago as the second member of the highly exclusive "zoo-panda club". New Yorkers responded overwhelmingly and, after eight hectic weeks of Pandora, an exhausted zoo patrolman was quoted as saying "Thirty thousand people asked me the way to the panda yesterday. Two men wanted to know where the okapi was, and a woman said she'd always wanted to see an aardvark."

*Pandora shortly after
arriving at the Bronx Zoo,
New York*

From the start Pandora had been referred to as a female and for once the identification was correct. Furthermore, when the Bronx Zoo set out to obtain a mate for her they managed to hit the right sex again. However, although they had been lucky with sexes, they were less fortunate with temperament. The new male, called Pan, weighed about 70 pounds on arrival (twice as much as Pandora when she made her debut) and was decidedly anti-social. Lee Crandall of the Bronx Zoo writes: "Pan was unlike the other young pandas received here in that he was unfriendly, even surly, in his reactions to his keepers. Although his weight increased from 72.5 pounds on arrival to 170 pounds at the time of his death on May 5th, 1940, he never adapted fully to captivity conditions." Pan had been caught by the same Chinese skin-collector, an ex-preacher called Den Wei-han, as had found Pandora a year previously. The animal was presented to New York this time by Mrs. Dean Sage, again with the help of the West China Union University, and reached the zoo on 1st May 1939. His short life span in captivity, therefore, was only one year and four days. Pandora outlived him by a year, dying of undetermined causes on 13th May 1941.

With the summer of 1941, New York found itself once again panda-less, and it remained so until the winter. On 30th December 1941, a pair of young pandas landed in New York, but they were the last to grace the Bronx Zoo and, indeed, the last to come out of China before the end of World War II. Their names, selected, as Lee Crandall put it, "through the sometimes unfortunate medium of a public contest" were Pan-dee and Pan-dah. They were thought to be a true pair and hopes were high that, as they were fairly well matched in weight (Pan-dee 62 pounds, Pan-dah

57 pounds), they would one day breed and provide New York with a zoo-man's dream: a panda family group complete with home-grown cub. A record first breeding of this species would easily have regained the prestige which New York had lost to Chicago over the Su-Lin affair. But their luck over panda-sexing had deserted them. Pan-dee was thought to be the male and Pan-dah the female, but when they died they both turned out to be females. The external differences which The Bronx officials must have studied were obviously individual characters rather than true sexual ones. Once again this is ample proof of the extraordinary difficulties there are in sexing this species, even when more than one animal can be examined at the same time.

With the political situation in China far from serene, the actual acquisition of Pan-dee and Pan-dah had proved to be a somewhat hazardous affair. Early in the summer of 1941 the Chinese government approached Dr. David Crockett Graham of the West China Union University with a request that he should do everything in his power to secure a panda for the wife of the Chinese leader. It was Mme. Chiang Kai-shek's intention to make a present of the animal to the American people in appreciation of their gifts to China through United China Relief.

Graham had played an important role in the acquisition of the previous two New York pandas, Pandora and Pan, and was the ideal person for the task. The ex-preacher Den Wei-han was contacted once again and he engaged two groups of hunters, one at Wei Chow and the other at Tsaopo. Between July and August the hunters made their first catch, but the animal fought loose and escaped. Urgent messages were sent to Dr. Graham pressing him

A prayer being offered to Mei Shan, the patron deity of the panda hunt, represented here by a flat slab of stone. (From Animal Kingdom)

to speed up the capture. He agreed to do what he could and went himself into panda country to help, but it was summer and the Chinese farmers were more interested in their crops. Also the vegetation was so dense at this time of year that it made hunting extremely difficult.

Dr. Graham gathered up Den Wei-han and together they toured the best panda centres, offering large rewards for live pandas. Seven bands of farmers stopped their work and trekked off into the hills. Eventually seventy hunters and forty dogs were out on the panda trail in seven different localities, and the biggest panda hunt in history was in progress. At Tsaopo they prayed to the hunter's god for success and a catch of three live pandas, promising him the sacrifice of a chicken and a pig if he answered their prayers. If he did not answer them, then they would whip him with sticks or throw him on the ground.

After some days Dr. Graham was able to buy a cub weighing 42 pounds from a local official, a Mr. Yang. He rushed back with it to Chengtu, arriving there on 30th September, although by this time he was tired, weak, and ill. A few days after his return, the hunters captured a second panda. Graham records that "While the animal was being pursued by men and dogs, one of the hunters ran up, seized it, and overpowered it with his bare hands. His clothing was torn but otherwise he escaped without injury." This panda, weighing nearly 60 pounds, arrived at Chengtu to join the first one on 13th October.

Graham, who was convinced that the first one was a female and the second a male, kept the "pair" carefully at his home in Chengtu for a month while waiting for them to be collected. During this time his house was virtually a panda "court", with a daily stream of visitors, including the Chinese governors of the provinces of Szechuan, Fukien and Shansi.

As an honoured gift from China to America, the two pandas were to be collected in person by John Tee-Van (an American, not a Chinaman, despite his name) of the Bronx Zoo. With the war in China going badly, Tee-Van had to make an incredibly roundabout trip, his total distance covered adding up to 34,868 miles by sea, air and rail. His outward trip went from New York via San Francisco, New Zealand, Australia, the East Indies, Singapore, Bangkok, Rangoon, the Burma Road and "thence to Chungking, war-battered but unbowed capital of China, and finally to Chengtu, ancient cultural center and capital of Szechuan province, where the pandas awaited me. Newly established war regulations made the journey an endless performance of labori-

Pan-dee and Pan-dah being carried up the 324 stone steps from the Yangtze River to Chungking. (From Animal Kingdom)

ously filling out documents, sometimes in sextuplicate, of supplying photographs and occasionally finger-prints". At Chengtu airfield "A decoy plane, made of bamboo covered with burlap and canvas, was mute evidence that the long tentacles of war reached this distant city." After collecting the pandas from Dr. Graham, a Douglas aircraft "brought us to the flagstoned runway of the mid-river island airport of Chungking. . . As the plane came onto the runway, swung over to the alighting place, and its door opened, the pandas were met by the shining nozzles of cameras. To the accompaniment of whirring film and clicking shutters, they were rapidly cleared through customs, placed on a sampan, ferried across the Yangtze-Kiang, and shouldered by coolies up the 324 steep stone steps to the Lin Sen Road. . . During the pandas' stay in Chungking they were visited by thousands and it was necessary to have three policemen on constant duty to control the crowd and guard the pandas. Only a dozen or so visitors had ever seen a panda before, for in China pandas are as little known as they are in America."

Shortly after their arrival in the wartime capital, the young animals were formally handed over. In a broadcast speech, Mme. Chiang Kai-shek sent the following message to the American people:

"Through the United China Relief, you, our American friends, are alleviating the suffering of our people and are binding the wounds which have been wantonly inflicted upon them through no fault of their own. As a very small way of saying 'Thank you', we would like to present to America, through you, Mr.

Mme. Chiang Kai-Shek inspects one of the pandas with John Tee-Van. (From Animal Kingdom)

The imposing giant panda passport instructing all officials to recognize Pan-dee and Pan-dah as gifts of the Chinese government. (From Animal Kingdom)

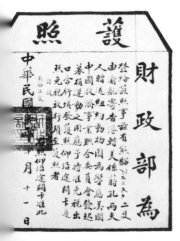

Tee-Van, this pair of comical, black-and-white, furry pandas. We hope that their cute antics will bring as much joy to the American children as American friendship has brought to our Chinese people."

The time was 4 a.m. The place was the bomb-scarred but newly re-opened radio station in Chungking. John Tee-Van suddenly realized that he was responsible for the safety not just of a pair of cubs, but of a symbol of international friendship. He had known this before, of course, but it was only now that the true weight of his responsibility dawned upon him.

On 14th November, complete with living clumps of bamboo, they took off to fly the 770 miles to Hong Kong, in a blacked-out plane and over Japanese held territory. Landing in a darkened Kowloon, alive with air-raid wardens, they bedded the pandas down comfortably at midnight. "A day later, pandas, bamboo and luggage went back to the airfield, which was soon to be bombed and captured by the Japanese, and were loaded on board the Hong Kong Clipper for the 758 mile journey over the China Sea to Cavite and Manila in the Philippines."

Pan-dee and Pan-dah were the first—and probably the last—giant pandas ever to set paw in the Philippines. Bamboo was forthcoming, but the problem was heat. Because of the state of the war the pandas were going to have to sail south, across the Equator, and then double back again up towards the west coast of the United States. The nightmare of keeping mountain animals with heavy pelts alive in the shimmering heat of the South Pacific was haunting John Tee-Van. "On November 27th, early in the

Pan-dee and Pan-dah on board ship, bound for the United States. (From *Animal Kingdom*)

morning before the intense midday heat asserted itself, and ten days before Japan attacked Hawaii, the pandas boarded ship at Manila to begin their long journey . . . On shipboard the pandas lived on the upper deck where breezes blew and where they could be kept as cool as possible. Except for the first four days out of Manila, when they almost died of heat and an intestinal disturbance, their health was perfect. Probably the only thing that kept me from jumping overboard in despair during those four days was the fact that I would have to write a telegram saying that the animals were ill or had died and I could not find the proper words . . . Midway of the voyage to Hawaii war began, and camouflaging of the ship was immediately started. The chief officer threatened to camouflage the pandas, for he asserted that their black and while coloration was entirely too conspicuous." One of the animals managed to achieve the desired effect accidentally by biting the legs of one of the sailors who was painting the camouflage markings on to the ship. In the chaos that followed, the characteristic starkness of the typical panda patterning became somewhat modified.

After a stop-off at Hawaii, the pandas eventually reached San Francisco without further mishap. On their way across the States to their final destination, they paused in Chicago just long enough for Mei-Mei and Mei-Lan to send them a little reminder, in the form of "cakes with super-imposed sugar-coated greetings of welcome to the newest pandas to come to America", that the Chicago animals were really the senior citizens where American zoo pandas were concerned.

Pan-dee and Pan-dah entered the Bronx Zoo on 30th December

Pan-dee and Pan-dah
together in New York.
(From *Animal Kingdom*)

BELOW:
*Pan-dah relaxes in
New York after the long
journey.* (From *Animal
Kingdom*)

1941. During the war they gave a great deal of quiet, escapist pleasure to New Yorkers anxious to have their minds taken off the grimmer matters of the early forties. Pan-dee died after nearly four years, with intestinal trouble, just as the world was emerging into peace again, but Pan-dah lived on into the fifties, succumbing after nearly ten years at the Bronx, on 31st October 1951. During the past fourteen years New York has once more been panda-less.

The only other American city to enjoy resident pandas, apart from Chicago and New York, was St. Louis. They possessed two specimens, a male called Happy and a female by the name of Pao-Pei. Happy was purchased from a German animal dealer on 24th June 1939, just in the nick of time before war broke out in Europe. Unlike most of the other captive pandas, he was a sturdy adult of 240 pounds when he arrived at the St. Louis Zoo. His age was unknown, but he resided there for nearly seven years, apparently

*Pan-dee startled zoo
officials by climbing a
hickory tree and refusing
to come down for 41
hours.* (From *Animal
Kingdom*)

97

living up to his nickname and quietly sharing his enclosure with his young mate Pao-Pei. The latter, brought from Chengtu to Hong Kong in the later summer of 1939 by Dr. Gordon Campbell, as a companion for Happy, weighed only 60 pounds on her first day at the zoo and the staff decided that the wedding would have to wait until the following year. By then, Pao-Pei had tripled her bulk and the introduction went ahead without any hitches. Pao-Pei was one of the best adjusted of all captive pandas, nearly rivalling Mei-Lan's longevity record. She lived in St. Louis for twelve years and nine months, dying eventually on 24th June 1952.

With the final deaths of New York's Pah-dah in 1951, St. Louis' Pao-Pei in 1952 and, last of all, Chicago's Mei-Lan in 1953, the dawn of 1954 saw the whole of the New World without a living panda to call their own. During the past decade there has been no change in this situation, despite one brave attempt to correct it that, as we shall see later, soon ground to a frustrating halt. With American-Chinese relations being what they are today, there appears to be little hope of the position improving for some time to come.

Despite Mr. A. T. Steele's predictions about pandas becoming a glut on the market there have, in fact, only ever been nine living specimens on American soil. All of these entered the states in a brief period of five years, from 1936 to 1941. Between them, they only spanned 17 years of American history, but during that time, they not only gave pleasure to millions of people, but also managed to launch a soft toy industry and inject a new animal image into the American way of thinking.

Happy and Pao-Pei at St. Louis Zoo

the London
pandas

the London pandas

CHAPTER SIX

Chiang Yee's fanciful version of the Tangier Smith pandas setting sail for London. (From The Story of Ming)

ONE NAME conspicuously absent from the last chapter is that of Floyd Tangier Smith. We left him, back in 1937, fuming at Ruth Harkness' success and avowing that he would soon be acquiring "bigger and better pandas" with which to startle the western world. He was dogged by set-back after set-back, but refused to give in. If we are to believe all the records, he managed to obtain the astonishing total of thirteen live giant pandas during his lifetime. This makes him the undisputed panda king, but thirteen is an unlucky number. From this whole assembly only four were destined to be successfully delivered and sold by Tangier Smith, and even then he was not able to enjoy his long-awaited triumph, for he was by that time a dying man. His first panda sales were his last and he succumbed to TB within months of completing the transaction.

From the outset his story was an unhappy one. Years of searching had failed to secure a living panda and then, in 1936, Ruth Harkness had marched in and walked off with the prize from the very heart of Tangier Smith territory. According to his own testimony he had even ear-marked the actual specimen for himself. Later, after securing two more, he lost them both, one dying at Chungking and the other at sea. After bringing other livestock to England in 1937 he returned to China and started panda-hunting with an almost desperate intensity. By the spring of 1938 he had caught no less than five, but one had already died. At Chengtu he now boasted three males and one female. By June one of the males had also succumbed, but further intensive collecting must have produced another five specimens because we know from his own writings that by the time he left China in the autumn he had presented two to the Chinese Government which "were the first live specimens in the Chinese Zoological Gardens" and had added three more to the two males and a female still surviving at Chengtu. With these six animals he set sail for England in the Blue Funnel liner *Antenor*. On the voyage one of the six animals died and yet another expired seventeen days after its arrival in London. The other four, however, were in reasonably good shape and at least enabled Tangier Smith to go to his death-bed with the knowledge that he had, despite his many losses and disasters, achieved the distinction of bringing to the western world the largest group of giant pandas ever seen alive (and, for that matter, ever likely to be seen alive).

The boat trip was comparatively quiet and restful after the chaos of the exodus from China. Tangier had already been a seriously sick man back in Chengtu. So much so, that he had been forced to call on his wife Elizabeth to take charge of the final stages of the operation: "On this occasion the difficulties of the expedition were complicated by the war in China. Instead of making the trip from the interior to Shanghai by river boat, we had to put all our cages and equipment on lorries and do a journey of 35 days to Hong Kong on roads that were often nearly impassable through bandit-infested country. I say 'we', but in fact I was ill and had to fly to Hong Kong while my wife took charge of the expedition. This was the first time she had gone exploring and much of my success was due to her courage and pertinacity. While my wife was bringing the lorries to Hong Kong, one of them tipped over and rolled down an embankment, setting loose two or three pandas. Happily they were quite willing to be caught again, and the incident led to the loss of nothing more than a day."

On board ship the pandas, according to a member of the crew, became friendly pets. They were chained to their open cages and spent a great deal of time lazing about on deck. Tangier Smith's health must have been badly in need of the sea breezes and deck chairs, but he had a whole collection of animals to look after, including rarities such as the blue sheep, musk deer, Szechuan marmots, and a young golden snub-nosed monkey. To make matters worse, they were heading into the dead of winter.

Dr. Geoffrey Vevers, who was then the superintendent of London Zoo, remembers the pandas' arrival vividly to this day. The *Antenor* docked in a snow-storm on Christmas eve 1938 and Vevers hurried across a tinsel-laden London in the freezing cold for his first glimpse of a giant panda. At the London docks he made straight for the *Antenor*'s berth and there, on the ship's deck, with the snow swirling around him, he saw the tall, gaunt figure of Major Tangier Smith wrapped tightly in a long fur overcoat and hugging to his bosom a tiny, golden monkey. The great collector hardly spoke. He was emaciated and obviously seriously ill. Vever's medical training told him that something had to be done quickly and he immediately started making arrangements to have Tangier Smith admitted to hospital. Like its owner, the little golden monkey—the first of its kind ever seen alive in the West— was riddled with TB. As the man was rushed to the Brompton Hospital, so the monkey was taken to the zoo's animal hospital, but neither survived. Tangier Smith did improve enough for his wife to be able to take him back home to the United States, but he died there after only a few months. For him the panda game was played out, but for Londoners it was just beginning.

At first the five pandas were kept behind the scenes at Regent's Park, while the zoo officials examined them and tried to decide how many to buy. There was an old female called Grandma who did not look too hopeful. She was refused and was still the property of the unfortunate Tangier Smith when she died of double pneumonia on 9th January, without ever having been seen by the British public. Then there were three other adults, a male called Happy and a pair called Grumpy and Dopey. Finally, there was a very young female panda called Baby, estimated to be under a year old and weighing less than 60 pounds.

The London Zoo eventually agreed to purchase the pair and the baby. Happy was sent to Germany on 26th January where he was sold to a German dealer and touted round the Continental zoos. He was the same "Happy" that we mentioned in the last chapter as being the first giant panda to grace the St. Louis Zoo in the

Happy at Leipzig Zoo
(From *Schneider*)

United States, but before arriving there on 24th June 1939 he covered a lot of ground. During his five months in a tortured Europe, with the war-clouds growing darker and darker, he was trundled back and forth between the major zoos of Nazi Germany, calling at Hannover, Berlin, Frankfurt, Munich, Leipzig, Nürnberg and Cologne. With World War II only twelve weeks off, the first travelling panda show in history came to an end at the Vincennes Park in Paris. From there Happy was moved to Cherbourg, where he once again boarded ship for a long sea voyage. Two weeks later he arrived in America and settled in his final home at St. Louis.

A giant panda in Paris. His exhausting German tour completed, Happy no longer lives up to his name at the Vincennes Zoo. (*Paul Popper*)

Happy retained his original nickname throughout his captive life, but the London Zoo trio were re-christened with exotic titles more suited to their oriental origins. The older pair became Sung and Tang, while the baby was re-named Ming.

Ming was first put on show at the zoo shortly after Christmas, but was taken behind the scenes again after only a week. It was the zoo's intention to keep her under special observation until she was a little stronger and then to launch her, like an animal débutante, when the zoo "season" got into full swing at Easter. But the zoo officials had reckoned without the panda magic. For any other animal this would have been an acceptable scheme, but the public, after only a week's exposure to the panda mystique, was not going to be fobbed off with a three-month wait. According to an *Express* headline: Panda Fans phone: "Don't hide him". Protests poured into the zoo. Hundreds of telephone calls jammed the switchboard and extra staff had to be drafted in to deal with them. The zoo was "overwhelmed" and a special meeting was called to discuss the situation. It was decided that the young animal would have to go on show again straight away, despite the risks involved, in order to satisfy the extraordinary public demand. But it was

Ming. The face that clicked a million turnstiles. (Photo by Suschitzky)

Ming with Alsatian companion provided by the zoo. (Radio Times Hulton)

agreed that she should only be exposed to the clamour of mass adulation for three hours each day—from noon until 3 p.m. The rest of the time was to be spent in the peace and quiet of the zoo's quarantine station in Camden Town. Every day just before midday a car was sent from the zoo to the station to collect the young animal. Ming was then driven in state to her specially erected enclosure in the converted tea pavilion.

As the days passed the crowds grew thicker and thicker. By February it was agreed to extend Ming's daily appearances by one hour. She now held court from noon until 4 p.m. By early March she had attracted an extra 7,500 people to the zoological gardens and her appeal was still growing. Commercial enterprises were being launched almost daily. There were panda postcards (£96 worth sold at the zoo within a few weeks), panda toys (almost obliterating the teddy bear for a brief period), panda novelties, panda strip-cartoons, panda brooches, and panda hats (made of white ermine with black fox ears and eyes). The panda craze that had struck Chicago in 1937 was now sweeping London.

As the cult proliferated, so the news of Ming's every twitch became stop press. The trivialities of her private life became as essential to Fleet Street as Hitler's rumblings across the Channel. It was eagerly announced that she was beginning to show signs of a romantic interest in the large male panda, Tang. He and his female Sung lived in the quarantine station alongside Ming and the young female had to pass their dens on her way to her public each day. At first she had growled angrily as she passed their cages, but now a change had overcome her. On 2nd March the *Telegraph* excitedly reported that: ". . . . she is making it clear that her anger is directed only against Sung the female giant panda. She pauses at Tang's den as if inclined to pay him a visit, and then she runs on, but looks back coyly and does not growl. Tang is definitely friendly towards Ming and it is hoped that they can be exhibited together. But the affair cannot be hurried."

In fact, the affair was never consummated and Ming died a solitary spinster. In March she weighed less than 100 pounds and was not yet half-grown. Long before she matured, both Tang and Sung had succumbed to London life, so that by the time she was ready to be mated, there was no-one to share her den.

Interest in the young panda had by now spread to the Palace and on 10th March it was reported that ". . . Ming gave audience to Queen Mary, the Princess Royal and Viscount Lascelles on Sunday afternoon. Detectives were present to see that Ming did not play any pranks. . . The Royal party actually went into the enclosure and Queen Mary asked whether it would be safe to fondle this amusing creature who had captured her fancy. When she approached, however, Ming, who has a fondness for human ankles, made a determined dive for Queen Mary's umbrella. . . Her Majesty laughed heartily at the incident, but she was even more amused when Ming, tickled on the tummy, 'giggled' help-lessly and covered her curious black-ringed eyes with her paws." With this, the adulation of Ming rose to a crescendo and vast queues formed at Regent's Park to snatch a glimpse of the sacred form. But across the Channel the news was becoming more and more sombre, and the frenzied interest in a small cuddly animal was sooner or later bound to turn someone's stomach. On 12th April Montague Smith threw up on the pages of the *Daily Mail* with these words: "The zoo visitors . . . have rubber-necked this monstrosity until their eyes ached. Nor does the matter end there. The sickly sentimental panda plague has infected far more people than can ever hope to see it in the flesh. Hundreds of thousands of postcard pictures of the panda are being sold and a recent film of its idiotic activities filled the newsreel theatres. Children are hug-ging panda dolls. China images of it occupy mantel pieces where formerly a not quite so hideous 'present from Margate' had the place of honour. Would-be fashionable young women are carrying panda mascots. Books, pictures, wallpaper, cigarette cases, jewellcry and jokes featuring the panda are making the lives of normal citizens hideous. And now the most nauseating of all symptoms of animal worship is making its appearance. The incorrigibly foolish are beginning to credit the panda with a soul."

The incorrigibly foolish were furious about this article and the *Daily Mail* was inundated with complaints. The most thoughtful protest came from a young boxer who commented that "There are so many brutal things about in the world today that it is attractive to find something that you can really have an affection for."

Montague Smith's objections were swept aside and as the spring of 1939 wore on, Ming continued to hold court at Regent's Park. On 10th May Princess Elizabeth and Princess Margaret visited the panda enclosure and all through the summer the pilgrimage continued. Sung had been sent off to Whipsnade in an attempt to attract crowds there too, and Tang had moved into quarters near those of young Ming in Regent's Park. Despite their large size, neither Sung nor Tang had the playful appeal of Ming and did nothing to diminish the smaller animal's hold over the public.

With ample supplies of fresh bamboo shoots coming in from all over Britain, Ming was growing rapidly. By August she weighed 150 pounds, three times her size on arrival. She was now so large

Ming visited by Princess Elizabeth and Princess Margaret in the spring of 1939

As a great star, Ming was forced to suffer certain indignities. This is probably the only panda ride in history.

that she had to be transported about the zoo in a wheelbarrow, as she was too heavy to carry and too destructive to the car that used to transport her.

On 18th August 1939 Ming appeared on B.B.C. television in

one of the earliest of all TV "outside broadcasts". There is little doubt that she would have gone on to become a great TV star, but exactly two weeks later she was being unceremoniously bundled on to a zoo lorry and carted off to Whipsnade, along with Tang and Ba-Bar, a baby elephant. War was imminent and the pandas were receiving V.I.P. treatment as priority evacuees. Two days after their safe arrival at the London Zoo's secluded country home thirty miles north of the city, war was declared.

After two autumn months at Whipsnade, Ming had put on so much weight that she was now nearly fully grown. In November Whipsnade shut its gates for the four cold months of winter and the three pandas enjoyed the privacy, the spaciousness, and the (for them) ideal climate high up on the Dunstable Downs. But even in these excellent conditions one of the pandas was weakening. Something was wrong with Sung. At first, it was thought that she must be hibernating, but later the authorities became alarmed and returned her to the Regent's Park sanatorium where she could come under the close observation of the zoo's pathologist.

Sung had always been a rather forlorn creature and had persistently refused to eat bamboo, feeding instead on cereals and porridge. Now she seemed unable to move about without great difficulty. During the first half of December, back at Regent's Park, she showed additional alarming signs, her whole body being shaken at intervals by convulsive movements. On the afternoon of 18th December Sung died. She was embalmed and sent to the Royal College of Surgeons for dissection. From there it was announced that the animal had some kind of long-standing disease of the spine, probably dating back to her days in China. The College also commented that the earlier panda death (Grandma) followed similar lines, and this inevitably makes us wonder whether these were two of the specimens that were thrown out of the crashing Tangier Smith lorry on the long trip across China. It seems reasonably likely that, as the lorry rolled over and over, the pandas were badly tossed about, and they may easily have damaged their backs during this episode.

Another statement from the Royal College of Surgeons echoed similar reports at American zoos. Sung had been wrongly sexed. She was a he. Little wonder that the zoo had found it impossible to keep the "pair" together.

Whereas the death of Grandma had been a private affair, Sung's demise was the first "public" panda fatality. This gave the press a new interest in the species and despite the fact that the country was on the threshold of a bloody war, grave notices were penned and sentimental poems composed. Part of one poem that was published on the day following her death reads as follows:

> *Sung, the Panda died today.*
> *At the Zoo she's lying stark.*
> *She'll be mourned in far Cathay*
> *And the wilds of Regent's Park.*
>
> *That's the message of the tapes:*
> *Sad-eyed Sung won't prank again—*
> *No more somersaults and japes*
> *To refresh the minds of men.*
>
> *Sung from China, peace to thee!*
> *'Tis a gloomy song I sing.*
> *Death hath taken one from three*
> *Left us only Tang and Ming.*

As before, the over-emotional climate led to some biting sarcasm. The following day an anonymous comment was made under the heading of "Dumb Friend's Corner": "Owing to the war the funeral of Sung, the Zoo panda, will be semi-state, we were told in Whitehall yesterday. The Island Race will be permitted to attend the lying-in-state at Regent's Park, but no mass demonstrations of public grief will be permitted. A deputation of representative modern thinkers will deposit a wreath and funeral orations will be delivered by Sloggers J..d and H.xl.y, dealing partly with the panda and partly with themselves. The notable silence of the Dean of Westminster is being freely commented on."

Ming, in the meantime, was going from strength to strength and by March had tipped the scales at 200 pounds. After a pleasant winter rolling around in the Whipsnade snow-drifts, she was now on her way back to Regent's Park to meet the Easter crowds again. With her return in mid-March came a note of uncertainty about her true sex. After the error with Sung, the authorities were presumably having second thoughts about Ming's femininity as well. (But in this case they need not have worried, she really was a she.) A month later, with Ming dutifully boosting the morale of wartime Londoners, the adult male Tang started throwing fits similar to those of Sung and Grandma and died after a short illness, on 23rd April 1940.

Ming was now alone, the sole panda survivor in the whole of war-torn Europe. During the next four years she became some-

Hope to see **YOU** at the **LONDON ZOO** soon

HE'S BACK! AT THE ZOO

L. R. Brightwell

TO SEE THE "OFF THE RATION" EXHIBITION AND YOU (AUGUST AND SEPTEMBER)

Wartime panda posters. In 1940 (left) the panda was depicted as a cuddly baby, but by 1942 (right) a purposeful, morale-boosting personality was required and Ming became Churchillian in appearance

thing of a symbol—a bit of fun in a funless, burning city. She was something exotically unreal in a epoch that was having its fill of reality. Soldiers visited her on leave, and she was shunted back and forth between Whipsnade and Regent's Park, according to the fortunes and misfortunes of the war in the air over London. Bombs fell on the zoo, but Ming was un-scathed. She was not, however, in the best of health. Her hair was thinning un-naturally and in the summer of 1943 she started walking backwards: "After lumbering around the cage in normal fashion she suddenly goes into reverse. Without troubling to turn round she retraces her steps backwards, continuing until she comes up against the rear wall with a bump." For a wartime symbol this is the kind of action that is hardly calculated to inspire the troops. Worse still: "When tired of this the panda sits at the bars and, facing the crowd, places both paws over her eyes." It was as if the great

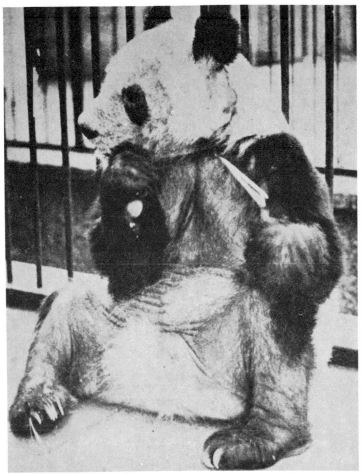

As the bombs fell, so did Ming's hair.

Troops of the Panda Division cluster around their mascot, Ming, at Whipsnade Park. (Fox Photos)

symbol was saying "I give up". This was in 1943. Early in 1944 the zoo wisely took her off exhibition and started a course of serious treatment in an attempt to restore her hair.

Every day Ming was attended by the zoo doctors who increased her vitamin intake, applied coconut oil to her thinning coat and sprayed her with "a special hair-nourishing liquid". Throughout 1944 she managed to hold her own, although she was said to be "dispirited and unwilling to entertain the public". Then, exactly six years (to the very day) after her arrival at London docks, she fell seriously ill. In a few days she was dead. Her keeper, returning from his Christmas celebrations, found her cold in her cage. The London *Times* published a non-satirical obituary of her, headed simply MING:

"Ming, the Panda, who made her first appearance at the London Zoo on Christmas eve 1938, died in her sleep on Boxing Day—she had been ailing for some time, and English-grown bamboos would seem to lack the vitamins of the Tibetan plant . . .

Ming, stuffed, as the taxidermist's centre-piece.

she could die happy in the knowledge that she had gladdened the universal heart, and, even in the stress of war, her death should not go unnoticed. . . She had the air of being the embodiment of some inspired nursery rhyme, and her proper habitation was less a prosaic cage than, in Mr. Walter De La Mare's words, 'some celestial happy medium between what is sense and what is non-sense.' . . . If there had been no panda we should surely have invented one . . . she will live in song and story as a fable, a superior kind of teddy bear become miraculously alive."

It would be pleasant to end her story here, on this note of passionate acclaim, but there is a sting in the tail yet to come. In January 1945 her body was presented to the Royal College of Surgeons and it was announced that it would be preserved in the John Hunter Museum where it could be made available to anatomical research workers. It appears, however, that this applied only to her internal organs for, as the war drew to an end in the spring of 1945, her stuffed pelt set off on a new career of making-friends-and-influencing-people. A large photograph of a taxidermized Ming appeared in the magazine *Illustrated*, with the following caption:

"Ming, the girl with the two lovely black eyes, is dead. But she's not lying down. Stuffed, she is travelling around the country carrying on with her job of entertaining the children. . . Recently she has been the centre of attraction at a big Liverpool store. Ming is quite a traveller and moves on to other places after about a fortnight's stay in one town. Ming, alive, was valued at £2,000. Her present owner, Mr. Gerrard of Gerrard's Natural History Studios, would not sell her. Ming, dead, is priceless." Such are the extraordinary contradictions of the world of the giant panda.

post-war
pandas

post-war pandas

CHAPTER SEVEN

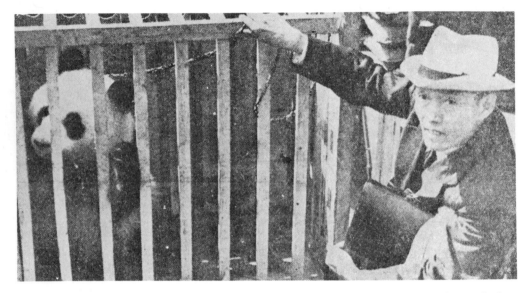

Ma Teh arrives in England with Lien-Ho, the first of the post-war pandas

THE CLOSE of World War II saw Europe once again panda-less. In an epoch of enforced austerity, of shortages, and peace-time ration-cards, there was a burning need for a few symbolic luxury items to brighten the dull routine. The London Zoo had no doubts about how it was going to solve this problem. It was obvious that a replacement for Ming had to be found and found quickly. But how? The old-time collectors like Tangier Smith had been swept away by the war.

The answer came unexpectedly over dinner one night at the Saville Club in Mayfair. Professor Edward Hindle, then Scientific Director of the Zoological Society of London, happened to mention casually to Dr. George K. C. Yeh of the Chinese Embassy that the zoo was seeking a contact to enable them to acquire another panda. Dr. Yeh promised to do what he could to help and dispatched an official letter to the Chinese Government.

His request was eventually passed to the governor of the province of Szechuan at Chengtu, General Chang Chun, who agreed to have not one, but a pair of giant pandas captured and sent as a gesture of goodwill and unity between Great Britain and China.

To repay this kindness, a rather unusual bargain was sealed. For each of the pandas the London Zoo agreed to provide a year's fellowship in England for a young Chinese biologist, all expenses paid. The university authorities at Chengtu were asked to select two suitable candidates for this imaginative offer and to prepare them for their special roles as panda chaperons. Dr. Kwo, the Minister of Education for the Szechuan Government, was inundated with applications from eager Chengtu University students. His number one selection was an earnest young lecturer in zoology, Dr. Ma Teh. If a second panda was caught, it was to be brought to England by a young botanist, Miss Hu Shih Yih, who had made a special study of the plants chosen as food by wild pandas.

Ma Teh was given the task of organizing the panda hunt and, with the thought of the London trip spurring him on, soon had half the local population out scouring the bamboo hills. Some reports claimed that there were over 200 people involved in the search. Panda territory was combed systematically by farmers and professional hunters in groups of ten, until at last an animal was sighted. It took two months of this intensive searching to locate and capture a young panda. For five weeks they saw nothing; then they made contact with one, but it managed to elude them. For a further three weeks they sighted it every day, but it always escaped. Then, finally, on 31st December 1945, it was driven into a tree by the hunters' dogs. When the men arrived, they surrounded the tree and began the delicate operation of lassoing the panda with a soft rope. To do this, one hunter had to climb a neighbouring tree with a long stick, to which was attached a rope with a noose. The problem was to get the noose over the animal's front legs as well as the head. If it fell only around the neck, then there was a danger that she might strangle herself.

The operation proved to be rather more difficult than was expected. According to Ma Teh, the animal 'was extremely intelligent. Time after time she caught the noose and threw it off her body'. Eventually she was secured and a second hunter climbed up to her, forced her down, and placed a bamboo muzzle over her face. The victorious party were then able to indulge in an extra-special New Year's Eve celebration.

Within a week the panda, now known as Lien-Ho (meaning Unity or Union, symbolizing the bond of friendship between China and Britain) had lost all fear of human beings and would come bounding over like a great shaggy dog when Ma Teh called her. She was transported to Chengtu in a specially built wooden crate. Once there, she became the centre of excited attention and the crowds flocking to see her reached such alarming proportions that she was promptly shipped back to Wenchwan, to be hidden away in a remote farmstead near the spot where she had been captured.

There she waited in quiet seclusion while all the complex details of her long journey were arranged and finalized. In the meantime the hunt was still on for a mate for Lien-Ho, but as the weeks dragged by the situation looked more and more hopeless and the farmers became anxious to return to their farms. After four months of disappointments it was decided to abandon the search and Lien-Ho began her marathon journey. Unlike the previous London pandas, she was to make the trip by air.

After being carried the seventy miles to Chengtu for a second time, she left there with Ma Teh in a special aircraft made available by Lieutenant General Sir Adrian Carton de Wiart, Prime Minister Attlee's personal representative with Generalissimo Chiang Kai-Shek. On 5th May 1946 the plane touched down at Chungking. Lien-Ho was in high spirits and ate a large meal of gruel honey and bamboo shoots. She was, however, suffering from the increase in temperature and was given a cool room with large fans to make her feel more comfortable. The following morning at dawn they took off again, this time heading towards real heat. The destination was Calcutta, where it was a sweltering 97°F in the shade.

Ma Teh became seriously worried about the panda's welfare, but to the rescue came Spencer's Ice and Cold Storage Plant. As soon as the animal arrived in Calcutta they installed her in a specially assembled cold chamber. There, with life-saving blocks of ice, Lien-Ho was able to sleep while she awaited the next leg of the journey. On a stretcher outside the door of her cold room lay Ma Teh, trying desperately to rest and keep an eye on the thermometer at the same time.

On the 9th May she was whisked out of her icy retreat and rushed through the burning heat to the air base at Bally on the Hooghly River. There her crate was carried by six Indian porters to a waiting motor-boat and raced across the water to a white B.O.A.C. Sunderland flying-boat. By this time the panda was panting hard and showing obvious signs of distress, but inside the aircraft was a reserved compartment amply supplied with massive slabs of ice, and the moment she was aboard she was let out to cool off. Ecstatically she turned over and over on what was virtually a floor of ice. B.O.A.C., who had at first refused to carry her at all, because of official regulations, had not only waived their rules in honour of their V.I.P. cargo, but had rolled out a special iced carpet and had saved the project from almost certain disaster. At 5 p.m. the flying-boat skimmed over the river and headed for Karachi, where the ice could be renewed; then Cairo, Marseilles and finally Poole harbour in the south of England.

For Ma Teh, B.O.A.C.'s thoughtfulness must have been more than welcome, but in Westminster reactions differed. According to one newspaper report: "The zoo's new baby panda, due to arrive by air next week, is causing a big stir. Should pandas be flown to London when 11,000 people are awaiting transport? Lord Munster has expressed indignation at the idea in the House of Lords. But neither the Air Ministry, the B.O.A.C., nor officials of the London Zoo are altering their plans. The panda, his bamboo shoots and his Chinese attendant will arrive in spite of Lord Munster." His Lordship was strongly criticized for his comments in the correspondence columns: " . . . it would have been tactless, undiplomatic and ungracious not to have provided a passage for this generous and imaginative gift from our great ally, China". But not everyone was prepared to put symbolic gestures before stark realities and back came the acid observation that, "The departure of Mr. Herbert Morrison for America on his mission to secure food for starving millions received less notice . . . than did . . . the Giant Panda with its supply of bamboo shoots to amuse the crowds at London Zoo." The British public were once again busy with their favourite occupation of putting animals before people and then hating themselves for it.

While this was going on, the Sunderland flying-boat was making steadily and uneventfully towards western Europe. On the afternoon of 11th May it circled the Dorset harbour and came to rest. Immediately tugs and launches filled with reporters, zoo men, photographers and officials of the Chinese Government converged on her. With cameras held high in the bobbing boats they waited poised to record the great moment, as if some notorious film star were about to descend from the plane's doorway. All they saw, in fact, was the handing out of a rather small wooden crate.

The crate was rushed to Bournemouth station where a special freight van was waiting, attached to a fast London train. A group of admirers, alerted presumably by radio reports of Lien-Ho's progress, were by this time gathering at Waterloo station, where she arrived in the early evening. From there she was dashed across London to Regent's Park in a B.O.A.C. van and delivered straight into the stores yard, where curators and vets were waiting to check her in. Passed as fit, she was taken direct to her large Lion House cage, freshly re-painted in a delicate shade of yellow.

This was, in fact, Ming's old cage and perhaps the zoo was hoping that some of Ming's earlier magic would rub off on the newcomer. But they were to be bitterly disappointed. Each panda has its own particular personality and Lien-Ho was no Ming. She proved it on her very first day by refusing to wake up the following morning and face her new public. They had been queuing for over an hour before the zoo gates were due to open and now, curled up in her sleeping den, she simply would not budge.

Lien-Ho keeps to the back of the zoo enclosure and avoids the crowds. (Radio Times Hulton)

After hours of coaxing by her new keeper, she finally confirmed her opinion of London life by biting him hard enough to draw blood. Eventually she was persuaded to put in a brief appearance for twenty minutes and was then thankfully back in her dark rear den again. Nor was this exceptional. Her surly and unhappy mood persisted and with it came a storm of protest. Had she gambolled and romped about gaily like Ming there would have been no adverse comment, but she was so clearly upset by her new form of existence that emotions flashed and flared: "Are we really a civilized nation when we hunt this little wild creature, the panda, take away its freedom and force it to be stared at in the Zoo, though it is so obviously thoroughly bewildered and unhappy?" asked an indignant correspondent in the *Express*.

Even royal visitors were unable to muster much enthusiasm. When the Duchess of Kent took her children, Prince Michael and Princess Alexandra, to meet Lien-Ho, the young prince was quoted as saying, "Not very big, is she? Have you got anything else new?", and they spent the rest of the visit playing with a common vixen. Asked for his views, her keeper could only comment: "She just sits there all day or sleeps. She only comes to the front of the cage when we lay a trail of bamboo shoots . . . people just don't seem to appeal to her."

In attempts to encourage her to more lively pursuits, a Whipsnade husky puppy was brought into the act, and a young boy was hired to keep her active. But the row in the press continued. "Panda plays as cruelty storm rages" shouted one headline. Apparently hundreds of protest letters were pouring in, but the zoo officials were unrepentant. They even emphasized that they were still going all out for a second one. For Lien-Ho, they announced, a new enclosure would be built in the form of a pagoda on the large central lawn.

Their continued concern for the welfare of the panda finally won through and shifted the public mood. *Punch* helped on 29th May by publishing a statement by Lien-Ho herself: ". . . One did not feel attracted to this new and vulgar civilization in the West, but it did one no harm. Anything was better than those awful hills, the Eternal snows, with their endless struggle for a livelihood. Here at least there were slaves to minister to one's bodily needs . . ." H. T. W. Bousfield added, in the *Queen* a few weeks later: "So frantic do the old women (of both sexes) become about our latest panda that I verily believe they envisage her as a nice young lady, brought up in a country vicarage of the best type, who has been kidnapped. If you explored their clouded minds further, you'd find traces of nursery stories of enchantment. Miss Panda, to them is, half consciously, an enchanted princess of sound Anglican principles."

By the summer Lien-Ho was settling down to the daily routine on the central lawn and was even lively enough by September to break down a small gate, march across a public walk, invade the zoo's First Aid Hut and terrorize the resident nurse, who was forced to defend herself with a broom and pail while the panda examined the bandages and ointments. With the arrival of autumn, Lien-Ho had discovered that she could climb high up into the top of her cage and lie there amongst the roof-struts, gazing lazily down on disgruntled humanity. For the next few years she lived on, sombrely munching her bamboo and snoozing aloft in the

High in the cage roof
struts, Lien-Ho gazes
down at the zoo visitors

Lien-Ho in the specially
built pagoda at the
London Zoo. (Radio
Times Hulton)

Political cartoon,
following a report that
Lien-Ho, alias Unity,
had been standing on its
head

bright light of day. In the music halls Flotsam summed it up with a poem which began:

> *I think I understand a*
> *Giant Panda;*
> *Why should she, while supplied with*
> *Bamboo shoots*
> *Give two hoots?*

The interest waned and little more comment was heard until Lien-Ho fell sick at the end of 1949. On 12th January 1950 she was admitted to the animal hospital seriously ill and underwent a course of injections. News of her condition appears to have reached the Nationalist Chinese Government. In *Time* magazine on 16th January we read that Dr. Cheng Tien-hsi, the Chinese ambassador in London, was summoned to the foreign office to hear from the Minister of State that Britain recognized Communist China and that the Nationalist Chinese Envoy was dismissed. Cheng and his staff were given three months to vacate the Chinese Embassy in Portland Place before the Communists moved in. *Time* comments: "He had one last ambassadorial duty to perform. On orders from Formosa, he gave £20 toward medical expenses for

Portrait of a dying panda. Lien-Ho in January 1950. (Radio Times Hulton)

ailing Lien-Ho, the giant panda presented to the London Zoo in 1946 by Nationalist China as a token of friendship."

The treatment failed and on 22nd February Lien-Ho died: "A keeper who found her sitting up in the sanatorium walked right up to her before he realized she was dead." In a bizarre way the death of this panda mimicked the death of the régime which had presented it. Like Lien-Ho, the Nationalist Chinese Government was effectively dead, but was still sitting propped up in the "sanatorium" of Formosa.

Hsing-Hsing in the Peking Zoo

Ping-Ping in the Moscow Zoo

The London Zoo announced that "we do not plan to replace Lien-Ho. Pandas, though a big box office draw, are perhaps best left in their native forests". Worried by the outbursts following Lien-Ho's arrival and her subsequently gloomy personality, the council of the Zoological Society agreed to put giant pandas on a zoo "black list" for all time. If they feared the loss of a box office species in taking this action, they need not have lost any sleep, for, as Lien-Ho's body was being taken away to the post mortem slab (where, almost inevitably by now, she proved to be a he), a tiny polar bear cub aged twelve weeks, called Brumas, was just being weighed for the first time. Within a few hectic weeks Lien-Ho was forgotten and Brumas was breaking all zoo records.

Three and a half years later, the last of the American pandas, Chicago's Mei-Lan, died and the dawn of 1954 saw the whole of the western world without a living specimen of a giant panda. With China still trying to sort out her massive economic re-organization under the new communist régime, panda prospects for the future looked bleak. Also, many zoos, like London, felt that the wild panda population was too small and valuable to be whittled down any further. But at this stage the Chinese themselves took a hand.

The information available from China is confused and confusing, but it seems that the new government started to take a serious interest in the Chinese fauna and the Chinese zoos, so that by 1955 the Peking Zoological Gardens could boast three young female giant pandas. Their names were Ping-Ping, Hsing-Hsing and Chi-Chi. By 1956 two more had been added, a female called Ssu-Mao and a large un-named male who died shortly afterwards. In July 1957 Ping-Ping was sent to Russia by Mao Tse Tung as a gift to the Soviet people and was given a new home in the Moscow Zoo. (She was to be followed later, in 1959, by a male called An'-An'.) Then, in December 1957, a very young female was caught by a team of animal-trappers in Szechuan and was moved successfully to Peking Zoo in January 1958. There she was looked after with great care by a Chinese girl and grew rapidly. Like one of the 1955 females this baby was also called Chi-Chi.

For several years an Austrian animal dealer called Heini Demmer had been trying to persuade the Chinese authorities to agree to release a panda in exchange for a collection of African big game. Peking Zoo was badly in need of re-stocking and Demmer's list, including as it did such things as giraffes and rhinos, was too attractive to ignore. They agreed that if he brought the animals to China he could select a panda and take it away with him.

Demmer and his wife left their Nairobi collecting station in April 1958 with three giraffes, two rhinos, two hippos and two zebras, and travelled to Peking via India, Thailand and Hong Kong, arriving in May: "The Director and all his staff were most kind and did their utmost to make our stay there as enjoyable as possible. The Zoological Garden of Peking is a wonderful park and has been rebuilt during the last few years in a remarkable way; it is now very modern indeed."

When Demmer was shown to the house containing the giant pandas he saw not four, but only three specimens. One, called Chi-Chi, was much smaller than the other two. It seems likely that the original Chi-Chi must have died and that its nick-name was passed on to the young newcomer in 1957. (This is a common practice with zoo nick-names.) Demmer records that "The Director was kind enough to give me complete freedom to choose one of their three pandas, which I thought was more than courteous. So, for about one week I more or less lived in this house and watched all three animals very carefully, and after a few days I made up my mind and asked the Director whether he would mind

Chi-Chi at Frankfurt Zoo meets actor Marcello Mastroianni. (Paul Popper)

if I accepted Chi-Chi, the smallest of the trio, but definitely the liveliest and naughtiest of them." The bargain was struck and Demmer and his wife took off with Chi-Chi in a Russian jet plane for Moscow. There they were greeted by the director of the Moscow Zoo who made a large compound available for Chi-Chi. In her new enclosure the young panda was rested for a week before making the next lap of her journey, to East Berlin.

Berlin, being a split city has two major zoos and Chi-Chi visited

Chi-Chi arrives in London. (From "Introducing Chi-Chi" Spring Books

both, her transfer from the East Berlin Zoo to the one in West Berlin being the most difficult stage in the whole journey. Or so it seemed at the time. But worse was yet to come. Chi-Chi had been provisionally sold to an American Zoo for the staggering sum of 25,000 dollars, but at the last minute the American authorities clamped down. The U.S. Treasury Department pointed out that as America did not officially recognize Communist China, there was an embargo on all trade with that country. Asked to make an exception in what was obviously an exceptional case, they flatly refused. The American zoo officials were frustrated and helpless. Demmer was stranded and dollar-less.

Frankfurt Zoo came to the rescue by offering to give Chi-Chi a free temporary home while Demmer continued negotiating, hoping, as he put it, that "some high person in Washington may close one eye and give Chi-Chi permission to enter and remain in the U.S.A., despite her communist background". But the high persons of Washington were unbending and in the end Demmer was driven to repeat a performance that had been the lot of the panda Happy and his owners twenty years previously. He started up the second great travelling panda-show, hiring Chi-Chi out to European zoos by the week.

Copenhagen was visited and then London. At Regent's Park the crowds turned out again to see the famous giant panda that had become the victim of international politics. For many, the

Heini Demmer struggles to give Chi-Chi her star-status bubble bath. (Fox Photos)

Chi-Chi escapes at London Zoo and Demmer leaps in pursuit. (Fox Photos)

Demmer carries the bulky runaway panda back to the zoo lawn. (Fox Photos)

127

memory of Lien-Ho was a glum one and they expected little. But they were pleasantly surprised. Chi-Chi was much more like the original Ming in personality and was soon sending out great waves of the original panda magic. She suffered the indignities of a bubble bath and provided ample copy for Fleet Street by escaping twice from her enclosure. On the first occasion she climbed over a low fence surrounding the lawn where she had been taken for photographs. On the second she scrambled out of her large pit while warm water was being tipped into her now famous tub. This time she managed to cause havoc by lumbering into a crowd of onlookers and biting a startled lady who was promptly rushed off to hospital, where she had three stitches in her damaged leg. Chi-Chi meanwhile was testing out her new hut, installed to give her shelter from the September sun. Her weight—122 pounds—was too much for it and it collapsed. For the onlookers, Chi-Chi was rapidly developing an attractively wicked personality, and the London Zoo started to think hard about the possibility of buying her.

In reaching a decision they had to consider two conflicting aspects of her case. On the one hand she was obviously a great attraction, and the crowds were so great that a specially enlarged circular platform had to be constructed around her enclosure to give more people a clear view of her. Also, if anyone was going to give her a permanent home, then it should be London, as that was the only European zoo with previous detailed knowledge of caring for this difficult species. On the other hand, the zoo's council had black-listed pandas for all time as being too hot to handle, and there was the difficult question of the large sum of money that Demmer was demanding for the animal.

Chi-Chi had arrived in London on the 5th September 1958 for a three-week visit and a decision had to be reached before that time was up, or Demmer would have to take her on to another zoo for another brief stay. After lengthy discussions it was decided that she must stay in Regent's Park, even if the cost was heavy. The orginal "no-panda" dictum had referred to attempts to take more pandas away from the wild state, but this specimen was already here. The London Zoo had in no way been instrumental in removing Chi-Chi from the wild. This had already been done by the Chinese, and the Zoo's real responsibility was now to ensure that the young animal had the very best possible treatment in captivity.

The financial problem was solved thanks to the assistance of the Granada television company, which agreed to pay the "lion's

The official handshake making Chi-Chi the property of the London Zoo. (Left to right: Heini Demmer, General Charles Dalton, Zoo Controller, and Dr. L. Harrison Mathews, Scientific Director.) (Fox Photos)

share" of the purchase price. The exact figures were never revealed, but according to Fleet Street the total price was in the region of £10,000. Chi-Chi became zoo property on the 26th September 1958, and Heini Demmer was able to breathe again. America's loss was London's gain and yet another panda epoch was about to begin.

The pattern was much the same as before and does not bear repeating in detail. There were television programmes, picture postcards, books, photographs and all the usual paraphernalia of animal stardom. A new 75-foot long enclosure was prepared complete with swimming pool, mist spray, weighing platform, suspended rubber tyres, and a pile of logs. Blocks of ice were placed in the enclosure on warm days for the panda to sprawl on, and the mist from the spray wafted gently down to cool her face. Behind the scenes there was a special kitchen where her meals were meticulously prepared, a bamboo store to keep her favourite food fresh and moist, an air purification installation to drive cleansed air through her indoor quarters, and her wood-lined sleeping den. A new keeper was taken on exclusively to tend to her minute-by-minute needs and to play with her when she became bored.

Chi-Chi eased herself gracefully into this life of luxury and steadily put on weight. She received royalty in the approved panda manner and relaxed. When there were heavy London fogs, she

Head Keeper Sam Morton keeps Chi-Chi busy while Oliver Graham-Jones, the London Zoo's veterinary officer, gives her a medical check-up. (Fox Photos)

A public appeal for bamboo by the zoo authorities brings an excellent response. (Fox Photos)

retired to her air-conditioned den and breathed more freely and comfortably than any of London's other ten million inhabitants. But she lacked one important ingredient in her life that they did not: a prospective mate. As the years passed and she approached sexual maturity, the problem became more and more acute. By the autumn of 1960, when she was just over three years old, she showed signs of coming into sexual heat for the first time. Her mood changed, she began calling and running around her enclosure, and she started to leave scent-marks on her "territory". She refused all food except the softest bamboo shoots.

The sexual mood passed, but returned in the spring of 1961 and again in the autumn. Each period of heat was a potential infant panda wasted and in January 1962 the Zoological Society sent an urgent plea to Peking asking whether they could help. In March, Tsui Chan-p'ing, the director of Peking Zoo replied, and we will quote him at length, as his comments provide us with virtually the only official statement, concerning current panda policy, to come out of modern China:

"As you will know, the distribution of the giant panda is extremely limited and in its natural habitat its existence is also limited by the particular natural conditions. Furthermore, in its natural environment, it suffers from the depredations of beasts of prey and, as you will well understand, its numbers may also have decreased since the development of communications.

"But from the establishment of our nation (The People's Republic of China), measures have rapidly been taken to protect the giant panda; regulations for the protection and hunting of it have been promulgated and put into effect. In order that the giant panda shall not decrease further in its natural habitat, hunting is prohibited for the time being, and for this reason we are at present unable to meet your wishes.

"We are confident that, thanks to the attention paid by our government and the research work undertaken by our zoologists in this field, the giant panda will not become extinct in its natural habitat."

And there the matter rested. The Chinese could hardly be blamed for their attitude. For years they had seen their panda territory plundered by westerners and now they had called a halt. If this seems unreasonable, it is a worthwhile exercise to imagine the roles reversed. Supposing a French priest, strolling on the shores of Loch Ness, discovered the Loch Ness Monster. Then suppose teams of Chinese hunters arrived and shot every Loch Ness Monster that they could find; following them, a Chinese lady who found a baby Monster and, without any official blessing, tried to get it out of the country to exhibit it in a Chinese Zoo; following her, more and more foreign collectors taking every living Loch Ness Monster they could find. It seems just possible that somewhere along the line the natives would have raised a faint protest against this course of events. Viewed through these spectacles, the panda scene takes on an entirely different appearance, and the Chinese emerge as unbelievably patient.

All this, however, was no comfort to Chi-Chi, whose periods of heat were becoming more and more intense, frequent and prolonged. In the autumn of 1963 she began a sexual phase that persisted for week after week. As she hardly ever ate anything when

Chi-Chi sits obligingly on the special weighing machine in her enclosure. (Fox Photos)

Large blocks of ice are provided for Chi-Chi on hot summer days. (Fox Photos)

she was on heat, the situation became desperate. Two months passed and she was beginning to lose weight. The zoo vet was called in and administered a heavy dose of tranquillizers. By mid-December she had calmed down and was munching away on her bamboo again as if nothing had happened.

In January 1964, the Zoological Society again approached the Chinese authorities, but to no avail. It looked very much as though Chi-Chi was going to have to face an annual round of heats and tranquillizers. In the spring, she scratched her eye on a piece of bamboo and was admitted to the animal hospital. Oliver Graham-Jones, the zoo's Senior Veterinary Officer, had the unenviable task of being the first person to be faced with the prospect of an-

Unlike Lien-Ho, Chi-Chi is a playful panda. (Granada TV)

aesthetizing a giant panda. Chi-Chi, valued now at £12,000 squinted at him from her cage in the hospital's operating theatre, as if defying him to calculate the correct dosage. With a deep breath he went into action and in a short while the western world's greatest animal star was sprawled out comfortably on the operating table. Everything worked perfectly and Graham-Jones was able to make good use of the opportunity to carry out a thorough medical examination of the animal. The eye was treated (and soon afterwards was completely healed), saliva and blood samples were taken, pulse rate was checked, and the fur was examined for any possible infections.

Most important, it was possible—perhaps for the first time—to make a close study of the sex organs of a living adult giant panda. After all the mistakes that had been made in the past, it was particularly interesting to see if anything definite could be established during life, given an anaesthetized panda. Chi-Chi had arrived at the zoo as a female and had always given the impression of being one, in her general behaviour. But back in August 1959 a famous anatomist had examined her as best he could in her zoo enclosure and pronounced that, once again, she was a he. He did not, of course, have a chance to examine her very closely and, in addition, she was still immature at the time. As she grew older, her keepers became more and more confirmed in their opinions that she really was a she. Now, at last, on the hospital operating table, it was possible to make sure. Animal breeding experts had been alerted and together carried out an examination that left them in no doubt. Chi-Chi, whose title apparently means "naughty little girl", had been well named: she was a she.

Chi-Chi recovered easily from her anaesthetic and by the next morning was active and lively again. Two months later, in June, she entered another period of heat and the zoo kept its fingers

Panda boy, Alan Kent, plays with Chi-Chi, watched by the Duke of Edinburgh and the Secretary of the Zoological Society of London, Sir Solly Zuckerman. (Granada TV)

crossed. But to everyone's pleasant surprise, she came out of it in little over a week. Just as it seemed that everything was back to normal, she shattered the peace in a completely unexpected way by savaging one of her young keepers.

Although she weighed 230 pounds and was no longer a playful cub, Chi-Chi had never been treated as a "wild" animal. All through her career at the zoo, she had had the company of her keepers, and they thought nothing of working in her enclosure with her looking on. Occasionally, during a bad spell of sexual frustration, she had become ill-tempered and taken a swipe at them, but she had never shown any signs of a really serious intent to attack them. Now, out of the blue, came this assault on sixteen year-old Christopher Madden. Chi-Chi had knocked him down and, as he lay helpless on his back, had sat on him and started savaging his right leg. Ken Alliborne, a keeper from the Monkey House nearby, heard his screams and without a moment's hesitation leapt into the enclosure (from which there was no escape for either man or panda) and ran towards the boy on the ground. Picking up Madden's broom, he tried as hard as he could to lever Chi-Chi off the boy, but she refused to budge. Blood was pouring from Madden's leg and Alliborne was forced to take drastic action. He clouted the panda on the head with the broom and Chi-Chi looked up, startled, just long enough for him to pull Madden clear. Chi-Chi then turned her attention to the newcomer and advanced threateningly towards Alliborne, her mouth covered with blood and mucous, growling angrily. Using the broom, he threatened back and managed to keep her at bay until help came and she could be shut away in her sleeping den.

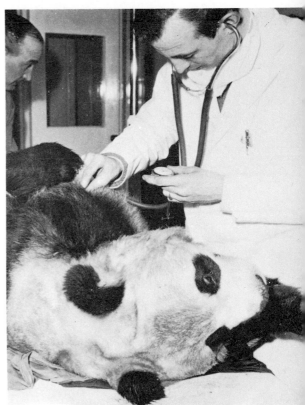

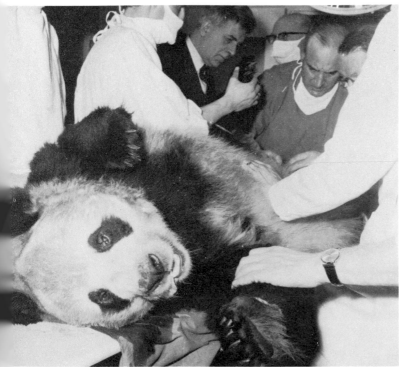

ABOVE LEFT:
*Oliver Graham-Jones
with a successfully
anaesthetized panda*

ABOVE:
*Chi-Chi sleeps quietly
on the operating table
while detailed medical
checks are made*

*At last Chi-Chi's sex
can be determined
beyond doubt*

Alliborne was awarded the Zoological Society's Bronze Medal for his bravery. Madden's leg slowly healed in hospital, while its owner worried about whether the zoo would let him have his old job back, working with the panda. Naturally the zoo was delighted, but Chi-Chi had other ideas. To Head Keeper Sam Morton's astonishment, she recognized Madden again instantly and started growling and pacing angrily up and down her enclosure as soon as the young keeper re-appeared. The strange feature of this reaction was that it took seven months for Madden's leg to heal sufficiently for him to return to work, so that, after knowing the boy for only a matter of weeks, Chi-Chi had remembered him as an individual after a considerable period of time.

Although this feat was a credit to the panda's intelligence, it meant that Madden's ambition to return to his old post could not be realized. Instead, he had to be transferred to another section and is at present working with the giraffes.

Chi-Chi now had to be treated as a "wild" animal. She showed little change in her behaviour, and there were no further indications of increased aggressiveness. In early September she started coming into heat again, but in a perfectly normal way. It was at this point that new hope dawned for the possible consummation of her sexual urges. Press reports from Moscow indicated that the zoo authorities there might perhaps be prepared to consider an East-

Giles cartoon in the Express, with the caption: "You realize that because of all this talk about Mr. Krushchev sending you a boy-friend from Moscow, Mao might have dropped a bomb on London Zoo."

West honeymoon between their male panda An'-An' and London's Chi-Chi. Immediately London Zoo sent the following cable:

"From press reports we are delighted to hear that you are interested in possible mating of Moscow and London pandas. We are happy to do anything to help this valuable zoological project. London Zoo officials prepared visit Moscow any time for discussions or we would welcome you as our guests here in London. We await your reply with great interest and hope that this will lead to greater friendship and co-operation between our two zoos."

In addition, letters were sent offering to have An'-An' as a guest panda in Regent's Park or to transport Chi-Chi to Moscow at the London Zoo's expense. Shortly afterwards pressmen in Moscow were told that there were difficulties and that the "manliness" of the Russian panda was in doubt. This led to a great deal of speculation and a variety of interpretations, some more serious than others.

It was suggested that perhaps An'-An' was sick, or that he was considered too dangerous, or that he was thought to be too valuable to risk in a mating attempt that might prove to be rather violent. In certain quarters it was felt that perhaps the Russians were not sure of the sex of their panda and were reluctant to admit this fact.

It emerged later that all these interpretations were incorrect. The truth was that the Moscow Zoo authorities were unhappy about the degree of isolation that both An'-An' and Chi-Chi had experienced during their adult lives. Neither had lived with another member of their species since they left China and it was feared that they would simply fail to respond appropriately to a panda of the opposite sex. The mating attempt was not on.

China came back into the picture briefly a few days later, when an animal dealer rang up the London Zoo and offered a Chinese zoo panda for sale. The price was a mere £27,500, including

Male An'-An' at the Moscow Zoo

*An'-An' as he appeared
on a Russian postage
stamp in* 1964

delivery to London. The animal was said to be available through a Chinese animal dealer, the only one who was permitted to enter and leave China freely without difficulty. The sex of the panda was unknown, but it was stressed very strongly that the animal was in good condition and that its export was entirely legal and above-board. This seemed very strange, after all the difficulties that had been encountered during the past few years, and London Zoo demanded official documents from the Chinese authorities before proceeding with any further discussions. These were not forth-coming and negotiations ceased. But the matter did not end there. News began to filter through that an American animal dealer was now offering a giant panda to the Los Angeles Zoo for something in the region of 100,000 dollars. Once again, its official status was stressed. Rumour had it that it was a 90-pound male and that the Chinese zoo involved was none other than Peking itself.

It is hard to know what to make of these fragments of inform-ation. Los Angeles reacted in the same way as London, demanding proof of legality. At the time of writing there is no further news of this mystery panda, but Los Angeles have promised that if ever they do acquire one they will be delighted to offer Chi-Chi a Hollywood honeymoon. At the present, however, they see "no real hope".

Early in 1965 An'-An' reared his head again. A report from Moscow indicated that he was showing signs of a sexual awakening and that Moscow Zoo might after all consider a mating for him with Chi-Chi. Michael Frayn in the *Observer* commented satirically: "Perhaps a long holiday together for the two pandas might be arranged. Friends of the happy couple believe they would choose Ibiza, or possibly Corfu, and mingle unnoticed among the crowds like any other holiday makers . . . Commentators in London point out that any meeting of the pandas would have to be preceded by a meeting at the tapir or wallaby level to prepare the ground . . ."

In fact, it seemed unlikely that Moscow was seriously re-considering the project, but London Zoo wrote again, to make sure, repeating the earlier offer.

At the time of writing, negotiations are still continuing and although hopes are slender for what is obviously an extremely delicate and difficult operation, London Zoo authorities are determined not to give up as long as both giant pandas are still living. By the time these words are in print perhaps something will have been achieved. (See postscript on p. 209-210.)

Chi-Chi's sexual cycles have happily shown no further compli-

The giant panda enclosure at Peking Zoo. (Photo by Ivor Montagu)

cations and she is now as healthy as she has ever been. A number of people have suggested artificial insemination as the answer to her problem, but although she would be easy enough to inseminate, someone would first have to collect some sperm from a male panda, and at the present time there is little chance that either the Russians or the Chinese would be prepared to attempt this.

For the time being Chi-Chi's story must end there, but the picture in Peking recently has been much more cheerful. Whether or not they have suddenly decided to sell off a young panda, one thing is certain. Namely, that they have made international zoo

Three pandas playing at Peking in 1956. (Photo by Chin Fu-Jen)

Female Li-Li and male at Peking in 1961. (Photo by Ivor Montagu)

history by breeding the species in captivity. They achieved this feat in September 1963, by which time they had had more than ten pandas under study in the zoological gardens, and had gained a great deal of experience. We mentioned earlier that in 1955 they had acquired three females, then another female and a male in 1956. In 1957 they obtained a young female called Li-Li who was destined to become the mother of the zoo-born baby. Later that year young Chi-Chi was caught and taken to Peking early in 1958. In 1961, when Ivor Montagu visited the gardens, he saw only one pair of adults, Li-Li and her husband. They had been living together amicably for some years, but without producing any offspring. Then, in 1962 a new male called Pi-Pi was brought in from the zoo's Animal Husbandry Station, where he had been living since 1959. Pi-Pi was mated up with Li-Li and this time the combination worked. At dawn on 9th September 1963, Li-Li gave birth to a 5-ounce male cub.

Ouyang Kan and Tung Shu-Hua, described officially as the pandas' "chief feeder" and "feeder" respectively, reported that: "We named the new-born panda Ming-Ming, meaning 'brilliant' in Chinese. Li-Li means 'beautiful', while Pi-Pi, the baby's father, means 'mischievous'." The birth was kept secret for three months because zoo staff feared a massive influx of visitors that might have upset the female panda.

The first zoo-born giant panda, Ming-Ming, cradled in Li-Li's arms

Li-Li proved to be a model mother, cradling Ming-Ming in her

141

Ming-Ming is carefully weighed by the Peking Zoo staff. (Photo by Pai Ying)

Ming-Ming growing rapidly

Lin-Lin being offered a banana by a member of the Peking Zoo staff

arms: "His mother at first held him on her lap or in her arms day and night, not putting him down for a moment, neither when eating nor when sleeping. After the first month, Li-Li became less anxious and permitted the keeper to handle Ming-Ming." Later, "When the baby was two months old, Li-Li would play with him by tossing him from one arm to the other. When Ming-Ming grew impatient, she would soothe him with her paw just like a mother caressing a child. At three months Ming-Ming could manage to walk. The world was a novelty to him. He frequently wandered away from his mother during her nap. Recently Ming-Ming has started playing alone outside his room. He wanders in the enclosure, nuzzling anything that comes his way. He forgets to return until his mother brings him back."

Almost exactly a year later, on 4th September 1964, Li-Li produced a second infant. Ming-Ming by this time was separated from his mother and growing rapidly. The new addition was a female and was called Lin-Lin, meaning "pretty jade". Rumour has it that the original male Pi-Pi, the father of Ming-Ming, had died, and that a new male had been brought in to provide Li-Li with yet another mate. If this is true, it strongly suggests that the so-called "animal husbandry station" connected with Peking Zoo is something of a major undertaking, able to whistle up the desired stock at short notice, even when the order is for a breeding panda. There are indications that the station is situated, not close to Peking, as some people have thought, but far off in panda country itself, most probably at Chengtu. With its long history as a kind of panda "clearing house", the University at Chengtu would be the obvious place to set up an organization for rationing out giant pandas to the various communist zoos.

This is, of course, pure conjecture on our part, for it is extremely difficult to obtain detailed information from China today. It is hard, even, to estimate accurately how many captive giant pandas there are, or have been, in Chinese Zoos (other than Peking) during recent years. When Ivor Montagu, a fellow of the Zoological Society of London, visited the Peking Zoo in April 1961, he was told that there were pandas in Shanghai, Nanking, Kunming (Yunnan) and Shensu. Between them these four zoos were said to have a total of five specimens, although it was not clear which one had two. This information was published in the *International Zoo Yearbook*, but Montagu later commented that Shensu should probably be written Chengdu. In 1964, Al Oeming, of the Alberta Game Farm in Canada, went to China and was able to see both Peking and Shanghai Zoos. He saw three giant pandas at each and was also informed that there was one at Pinkiang (Harbin) in the north-east and a trio at Chengtu. It seems likely that Shensu, alias Chengdu, is in fact Chengtu, but we cannot be certain of this.

Information also reached the office of the *Zoo Yearbook* in 1964 that two captive giant pandas had been seen that year, down in the south of China, in Canton Zoo, where a great deal of re-building and development was in progress. All over China, it seems, re-construction and modernization of zoological gardens is actively under way, and we can certainly expect to hear of more captive pandas and more panda breeding successes in the near future. Perhaps one day China will feel sufficiently confident of the biological status of their unique panda population to be prepared to release a few breeding pairs to the rest of the world. Until such a time, Chi-Chi in London and An'-An' in Moscow will have to suffice as isolated reminders of the flesh-and-blood existence of this marvellous and extraordinary creature.

Li-Li with her second offspring, Lin-Lin

the panda as an animal

the panda as an animal

CHAPTER EIGHT

Styan's panda, the large Chinese race of the red panda

DESPITE its colourful history, we know remarkably little about the biology of the giant panda or, for that matter, about the biology of its small cousin, the red panda. Both animals await detailed field studies by professional zoologists, and when one looks at the "field" in question it is not hard to see why. They inhabit such inhospitable regions that it will be a brave man indeed who eventually sets out to unravel the secrets of their daily lives. But we are not completely ignorant. Scraps of information, a bit from here and a piece from there, have become available over the years and we can glean some idea of their natural existence by assembling these hard-won fragments. In addition we can supplement the picture with certain facts learned from the behaviour of captive specimens and from the anatomical studies made of dead pandas.

Firstly, where do they live? It has already emerged that they are confined to the Himalayan region of Central Asia, but what is their exact geographical range? The red panda covers a wider area than the giant, being found all along the forested slopes of the Himalayan Mountains, through Nepal, Sikkim, northern Burma and into Western China. At the eastern end of its range it becomes larger and sturdier, and this Chinese race is known as Styan's panda (*Ailurus fulgens styani*) after the man who discovered it in 1897, F. W. Styan. It is found right through northern Yunnan and up into Szechuan, almost to the borders of Kansu. Its distribution therefore overlaps considerably with that of the giant panda.

Both species live at high altitudes, typically between 5,000 and 10,000 feet, but the red panda is said to extend even higher, to as much as 12,000 feet.

The stronghold of the giant panda is undoubtedly Szechuan, but there are a few isolated observations indicating that it extends well beyond the borders of this province of western China. The Russian explorer Berezovski, approaching panda country from the north, encountered it in the southernmost regions of Kansu, in the mountain range that forms the border between Kansu and Szechuan. This is nearly 500 miles north of Yehli, where the Roosevelts shot their giant panda. Yehli itself is also outside the Szechuan area, being south of the Tung River in eastern Sikang.

Sowerby claims that the animal's range even extends to the borders of Yunnan in the south and to the southern edge of Shensi in the north. If this is really the case, then it is no longer possible to refer to the giant panda's Chinese distribution as "very restricted". The area covered by the species must amount to many thousands of square miles. Furthermore, there is recent reliable evidence that the giant panda occurs beyond the borders of China itself. Hung-Shou Pen, along with other members of a Natural Resources Exploration Expedition, encountered a mother with two cubs far away to the west, on the Tibetan plateau. It was early morning on 10th June 1940, when they saw them. The party was near the twin lakes of Tsaring Nor and Oring Nor in the Chinghai province of north-eastern Tibet. The expedition guide was the first to spot them, sauntering along on the opposite side of a river. The explorers quickly forded the river on horseback and were then able to watch as the mother panda munched her breakfast. "The colour of the two cubs was paler than that of the mother animal. They followed and sucked their mother as does a little pig or calf. Later they turned back and suddenly flashed before us in all their beauty. Our guide and bodyguards drove them away by shouting. They were then frightened and hurried away."

Hung-Shou Pen was naturally excited about this observation, since the nearest known giant panda country was over 175 miles away to the east, and he began to make enquiries to try and

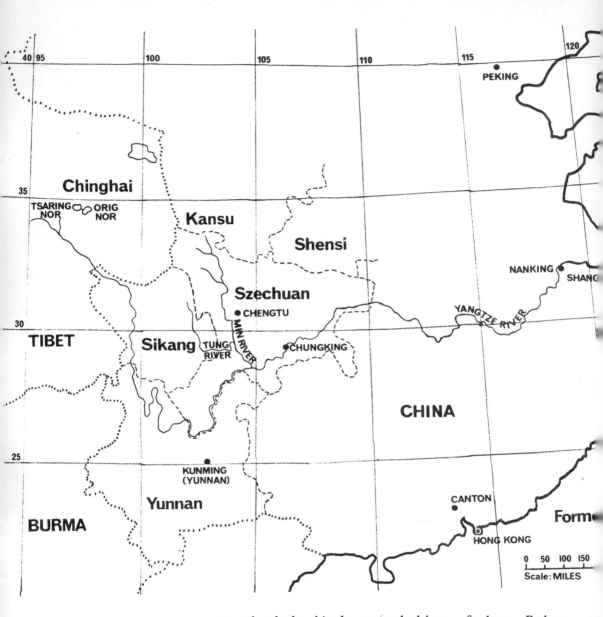

ascertain whether his observation had been a freak case. Perhaps these animals were isolated, displaced pandas, a long way off their normal beat. But this did not appear to be the case. He was informed that: "The fur of the panda is rarely to be found in the market at Sining, the capital of Chinghai province. It does not fetch such a good price as that of the blue bear, as the fur is considered rather coarse." In other words, pandas were well known enough in Tibet for the qualities of their fur to be weighed against that of the local bears. Without any doubt, the species has a Tibetan population in addition to its more famous Chinese one.

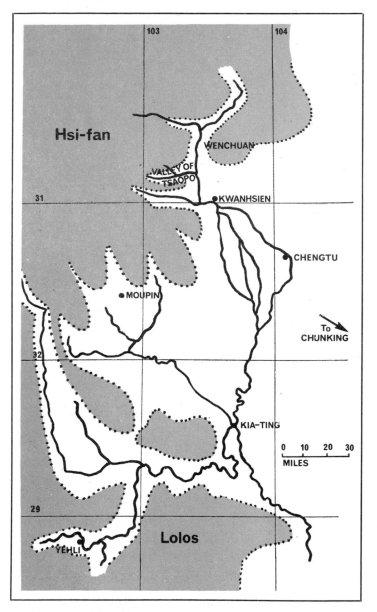

Altogether this adds up to a formidable Asiatic distribution, extending from Chinghai in the north-west to Shensi in the north-east to Yunnan in the south, making a triangle with 500-mile sides. (Approximate maximum longitudes: 97°–107°; approximate maximum latitudes: 27°–35°.) As there are many unexplored mountainous regions adjacent to this area, we may yet see the panda's territory expand still further in the textbooks of the future.

As we have seen from earlier chapters, the typical giant panda habitat is the almost impenetrable bamboo forest on the steep mountain slopes. This bamboo belt gives way, higher up, to the rhododendron forest, and into this the animal does not normally venture. Only two exceptions to this rule were noted by the members of the Sage West China Expedition: "In one case we found unmistakable panda droppings high on the Chen Lliang Shan range, 1,000 feet above the rhododendron forest, and probably 1,500 feet above the nearest bamboo. It was interesting to find that on occasion the panda must travel above its regular habitat to the bare grasslands of the blue sheep country. In another instance I saw where a giant panda had climbed a small pine tree just above the village of Tsapei on Chengou River. It was located 300 feet above the river bottom on an open slope, with the nearest bamboos across the valley."

Hung-Shou Pen's Tibetan observation is, of course, another exception, for he saw his animals on the open steppe of the high plateau. The mother panda was clearly seen to be feeding on a variety of succulent plants that were plentiful at the time. Pen argues that perhaps there is an annual east-west panda migration, determined by the fluctuating food supplies. He points out that in the winter the plateau would be too bleak and the animals would descend eastwards to the bamboo slopes of the mountains, across the border in western China. There they would spend the winter months and then trek back to the west again at the end of the following spring: "This westward migration will lead the animal through an open valley where the Ma Chu or the uppermost part of the Yellow River passes through. Along this stream there is a great abundance of water and vegetables. The winter and spring are severely cold on the plateau; while in the forests of the high mountains the weather is less rigorous and bamboo shoots are thickly growing and provide the panda with its staple food. In the summer the conditions are reversed in these two habitats: in the plateau nutritious vegetables are to be found everywhere, besides a plentiful supply of mouse-hares and fishes. At that time the accumulated snow in the forests is still there unmelted and the succulent bamboo shoots have already grown into bamboo thickets no longer palatable. Other vegetables are covered by snow as on the plateau in winter. That is the reason why the panda has to migrate to the Tibetan plateau in summer."

Although this is an ingenious idea it is perhaps dangerous to accept it too readily on the basis of Pen's slender information. It may well apply to those pandas living near the Tibetan border, but it is doubtful if all the Chinese specimens from further east set off on a regular summer migration of this kind.

The most important aspect of Pen's report is that it proves something about wild pandas that zoo men had already discovered with their captive specimens, namely that they can survive—for a while at least—on a completely bamboo-less diet. Strangely enough this fact is mentioned by Père David in the very first published notes on the giant panda's way of life, but seems to have been overlooked by later writers. They were so absorbed by the bamboo-eating specializations of the species that they automatically assumed it ate nothing else. It was Sheldon who finally sealed the error in 1937, with his authoritative statement that "Not only is the giant panda entirely herbivorous, but it is known to live on the dwarf bamboo of the northeastern spur of the Himalayas to the exclusion of *all* other vegetable matter." From that date onwards the giant panda was looked upon as a totally bamboo-bound species, like the koala in its gum trees, but Hung-Shou Pen's female panda was happily tucking in to gentians, irises, crocuses, Chinese vines (*Lycium chinense*), and tufted grasses such as ticegrass and bent-grass. The plants were apparently grubbed up by the female who then ate them, roots, bulbs, leaves, and all.

The local Tibetan inhabitants claimed that the giant panda also occasionally hunted fish, pikas (mouse-hares) and small rodents, but Pen was unable to back this up with personal observations. Père David had been told a similar story seventy years before: "It is said that it does not refuse meat when the occasion presents itself." It is surprising therefore to read in Dwight Davis' monograph in 1964 that "They refuse meat in captivity." It is not only surprising, it is also untrue. Chi-Chi has been luxuriating on morsels of roast chicken as a diet supplement ever since she arrived in London in 1958.

Despite these comments it must be admitted that bamboo *is* the principal, basic diet of the giant panda and it is interesting to see just how the animal deals with such an unfriendly food. The bamboo in question goes by the name of *Sinarundinaria* and it grows in dense thickets to a height of 10 to 12 feet. The culms are slender, rarely exceeding an inch-and-a-half in diameter. Naturally, the panda prefers the thinner, younger and more succulent shoots to the older, tougher stems, but these alone would be insufficient for its needs. In addition it breaks off the bigger, hardened culms and devours these too. By examining the remains of panda feasts in the field, Ernst Schaefer was able to conclude that "The bulk of its nourishment consists . . . of stone-hard bamboo stems thicker than a finger. With its powerful molar teeth the panda bites off the 3 to 6 m. long stems about 20 to 40 cm. above

The feet of a giant panda compared with those of a bear. (A: panda, front left. B: panda rear left. C: bear front left. D: bear rear left. The arrow points to the "sixth claw". (After Dwight Davis)

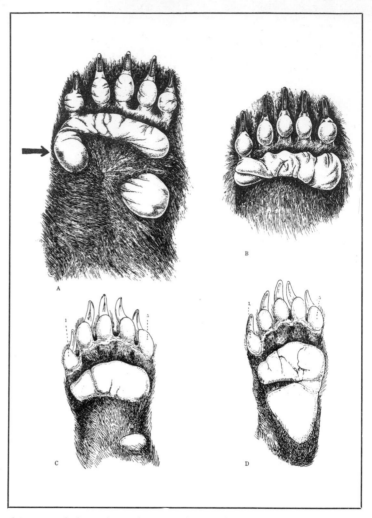

the ground, lays them down and eats the middle part up to the beginning of the leaves, while it regularly rejects the lower, hard part and lets it lie. Such chewed places are not particularly hard to find, although they are always concealed in the middle of the jungle. Usually they are not larger than one to two square metres. In these places perhaps 15 to 20 stems are bitten off, and the rejected parts cover the ground."

In the act of eating the giant panda brings into play its specialized front feet. We have already referred to the famous "sixth claw" that enables it to grasp with precision even the most slender stalks and carry them to the mouth. This is not really a claw at all, but an elongated wrist-bone (35 mm. in length) covered in a tough, fleshy pad. It functions exactly like an opposable thumb. For some reason the real thumb was not employed in this evolutionary development. It lies quietly alongside the other four digits and

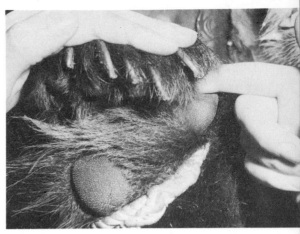

When Chi-Chi was anaesthetized in the London Zoo hospital it was possible to obtain these pictures of her front foot in the open and clasped positions. The human finger represents a stick of bamboo. (Zoological Society of London)

acts *with* them, not against them as in man. The mobility of the panda's pseudo-thumb is not passive. It is capable of active, powerful grasping, thanks to the fact that during the course of evolution it has stolen some of the muscles normally running to the real thumb. These have shifted over and become attached to the enlarged wrist-bone, endowing it with powerful "opening" and "closing" movements that provide the hand of the panda with a strong forceps grasp.

The pseudo-thumb bone is known technically as the radial sesamoid and it is interesting that this same bone is also enlarged, but not to such a great extent, in the red panda. This animal can also use it to grasp bamboo shoots, but there is obviously less power involved. It would seem that, as the giant panda grew bigger during the course of evolution, and began to feed on larger and tougher stems of bamboo, its grasping mechanism managed to keep pace by becoming more and more sturdy and muscular, until it developed into the unique pseudo-thumb that we see to-day. Throughout the whole animal kingdom there is nothing exactly like it.

Having this dextrous ability, the giant panda can sit back and enjoy its meal in a relaxed posture. In fact, it always carries the

Typical feeding posture. The giant panda sits in a relaxed position, bringing the bamboo stalk up to its mouth. (Granada TV)

bamboo up to its mouth, rather than lowering the mouth to the food. In this way its feeding movements and postures are superficially extremely human.

When the bamboo stalk is brought up to the mouth, it is grasped by the teeth and the tough outer layers are stripped off. This is achieved by a sideways turning of the head combined with a twisting movement of the hand. The peeled stalk is then placed sideways into the corner of the mouth, where the massive cheek teeth lie. With a powerful crunch of the heavy jaws a section is then bitten off and laboriously chewed.

The whole head of the giant panda has become modified as a crunching machine. The skull is heavy, the jaws broad and strong, the muscles immense. The cheek teeth are huge, blunt, grinding-stumps. They are adorned with so many ridges and tubercles that drawings of them look like miniature relief maps of the mountainous terrain in which the animal lives.

Even after being battered by the mighty molars, the swallowed bamboo fragments are still formidable objects for any digestive tract to have to deal with. It is not surprising to find that the oesophagus has a horny lining, or that the stomach is thick-

Even a small piece of bread can be held easily in the clasped hand. (Granada TV)

walled, muscular and almost gizzard-like. The panda does, however, have a surprise in store for us in its guts. The prediction here would have been that the intestines would be tremendously elongated. This is typically what happens with other herbivorous mammals. But with the giant panda (and the red panda, too, for that matter) the guts are shortened instead of lengthened. This secondary shortening of the intestines connected with a secondary herbivory is as odd and as unique as the panda's pseudo-thumb.

The total length of the unwound intestines of an adult giant panda is only five-and-a-half times its overall body length. In relative terms, this makes it one of the shortest-gutted carnivores in the world today. When one thinks of the indigestible nature of its bamboo diet, it is hard to understand why there has not been some elaboration of the guts to help deal with the situation. A close look at the different sections of the intestines reveals that most of the shortening has taken place in the region next to the stomach and it has been argued that, at this stage, the food is still largely insoluble. It is thought to be passed quickly through the abbreviated small intestine and on into the comparatively normal large intestine, where it can be acted upon by the gut bacteria and protozoa.

The strange thing about the panda's digestive system is that it is obviously so inefficient that one would think it had only just started to evolve and was not yet properly adapted to the newly acquired plant-eating habits of its originally carnivorous owner. But then one has to cast one's mind back to the extraordinarily efficient development of the bamboo grasping pseudo-thumb. It can hardly be said that that organ is "just beginning" to develop. And so, for the present, the giant panda's guts must retain their mystery.

One point is certain, namely that they do not retain much of the goodness of the swallowed bamboo. Field observers have always reported that the droppings of giant pandas are remarkable for their size and for the largely undigested matter they contain. William Sheldon managed to make reasonably detailed observations in one particular case, when he was able to follow the track of an adult animal for some distance, shortly after snow had fallen: "For two miles it wound in and out through the bamboo thickets where the animal had fed, and the surprising detail was that at an average of every hundred yards there were from one to three large droppings (4 to 6 inches long and 2 inches thick, tapering at each end). At a conservative estimate there were 40 droppings when the track was still two hours old. At this point I disturbed the panda, but could not see it because of the dense bamboos. The animal had been resting at the base of a small spruce tree, and must have stopped feeding before 9 a.m. Below the resting place was a pile of at least 30 more droppings, making a total of 70 excreted between the very early morning and 9 a.m. . . . I pursued the animal for three hours longer, and I found droppings almost as frequently for another four miles, although it had not stopped to feed meanwhile. . . These droppings emerge almost totally undigested. It seems logical to assume that an animal of such large proportions must have to eat tremendous quantities to secure the nourishment that it requires. . . I estimate that they would have to spend from 10 to 12 hours a day feeding in order to secure sufficient for their needs."

The panda in the wild state is therefore a giant food machine of rather poor quality, like the gorilla. Surrounded all day by its natural bamboo larder, it sits munching steadfastly on, hour after hour. Its more lethal relatives—the carnivorous carnivores—would, if they understood, sneer at it as a clumsy, heavy-boned, dim-wit. Instead of hunting down highly nutritious prey every so often and then lying around sunning itself, the panda has waved goodbye to the nimble-minded world of helter-skelter chases, bloated blood-feasts and sprawling cat-naps. Instead it has become (literally) a manual labourer, toiling endlessly at its repetitive bamboo-picking tasks.

In reply, the panda would no doubt point out that life in the bamboo forests is serene and untroubled by sudden deaths and disasters. There are no predators to speak of, and an endless supply of food. If one has to be heavy-boned and clumsy in order to crunch it up, it really does not matter, because there is nothing to force one to be un-clumsy. There is no pressure on one to start sprinting, either towards a prey or away from a predator. Life in the bamboo jungle has its compensations.

Moving from wild pandas to zoo-kept specimens, it is not surprising to find them taking greedily to nutritious diet substitutes. With their inefficient digestive systems, a carefully prepared "porridge" of mixed fruits, vegetables, cereals, minerals and vitamins soon proved most welcome and drastically cut down the amount of time spent feeding. It did not always cut it down enough, however, and some pandas tended to gorge themselves on this new luxury diet and rapidly became over-weight. In some instances they even began to ignore their ancestral bamboo. Zoo officials decided that the only thing to do was to ration the rich substitutes and insist that their pandas ate at least half their daily food in the form of bamboo shoots and stems. This system has worked well ever since and, in the main, the feeding of captive pandas has provided less of a problem than was once feared.

Shortly after Chi-Chi had been purchased by the London Zoo, the veterinary department instituted the following daily food régime for her:

1 lb. boiled rice	½ lb. bread
6 oranges	yeast
6 bananas	sugar
3 pears	salt
3 apples	chicken (cooked, every other day)
grated carrots	vitamin additives
2 eggs (raw)	mineral additives

Half this daily diet was mixed up into a "porridge" and served in the morning. The other half was mixed and served in the evening. The total daily weight of this food was between 9 and 10 pounds. A constant supply of bamboo was also available, with a minimum of 9 pounds put into the panda's enclosure every day.

At the time when this feeding régime was introduced Chi-Chi weighed about 150 pounds. On the average she consumed about 9 pounds of the porridge and 6 pounds of bamboo every day through her first winter at the zoo. As the months passed and she began to grow, the amounts offered were modified slightly and the components of the porridge were somewhat simplified, but the basic system was retained and has proved successful ever since. At one point, Chi-Chi did start to become over-weight and it was then that the "fifty-per-cent-bamboo" diet rule was enforced. When she became mature, however, and started to experience her first periods of heat, it was the porridge and not the bamboo that fell out of favour. This is an interesting twist in food preferences. Previously she had been only too eager to demolish her special mixture and, as with other pandas, she was in danger of becoming de-bambooed. But now, with her food intake sinking lower and lower as the sexual mood increased, it was the porridge that was the first to be ignored. At the height of the sexual heat, nothing at all was eaten, but just before and after the peak she would still toy with a bunch of bamboo shoots. It is hard to explain this shift in preferences and we are once again up against the hard fact that we really know next to nothing about the natural feeding habits of the animal. Perhaps there *are* seasonal changes in the kinds of food preferred, as Penn has suggested. In the meantime it is worthless to speculate. We must simply wait patiently for the Chinese to make a detailed field study.

In American Zoos the feeding régime has been much the same as at London, with a few minor differences. At Chicago, Robert Bean offered his pandas vegetables, fruit and sliced bread in addition to bamboo. His diet included green corn stalks, green soy bean plants, spinach, chard, raw carrots, apples, milk and porridge. At New York, Pandora was at first also given a wide variety of supplements, including milk, egg, honey, orange juice, fish oil, green corn stalks, willow sprigs, celery, lettuce, chard, beet tops and baked potato. After a while she began to refuse many of these items and by the time she was adult was only taking bamboo and a semi-liquid formula consisting principally of powdered milk, raw eggs, honey, water, and vitamin and mineral additives. Again, one would like to know the exact significance of this change in food preferences, but again we can only record it and await further news from China.

At Peking Zoo the food régime for pandas appears to be much the same as in the West. In addition to bamboo leaves and shoots they are given milk, sweetened gruel, eggs and biscuits, three times a day.

Turning from feeding to breeding, the evidence is even more fragmentary, but we do have certain brief details from Peking concerning their two successful giant panda births. Both occurred at the beginning of September, Ming-Ming appearing on 9th September and Lin-Lin on 4th September the following year. The most astonishing fact to emerge is that Ming-Ming weighed no more than 5 ounces at birth and looked rather like a small rat... "One could scarcely recognize him as a giant panda." His mother Li-Li, at 250 pounds was 800 times as heavy as her offspring.

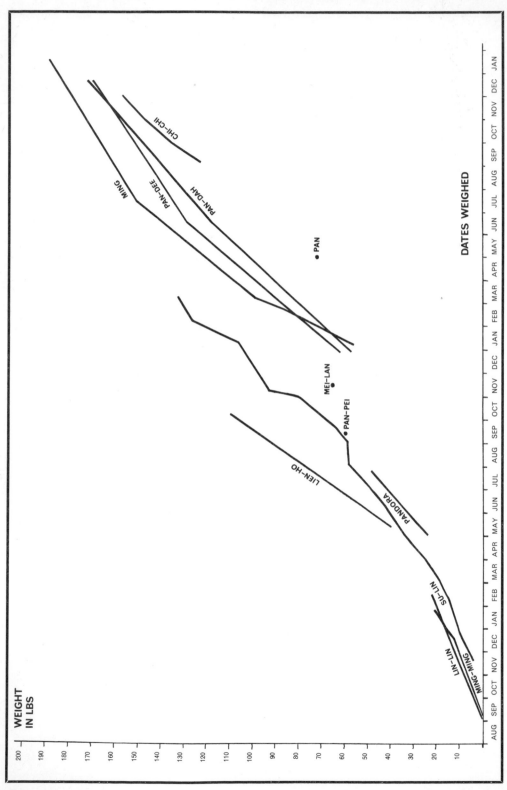

WEIGHT
IN LBS

DATES WEIGHED

CHI-CHI

PAN-DAH

PAN-DEE

MING

PAN

MEI-LAN

PAN-PEI

LIEN-HO

PANDORA

SU-LIN

LIN-LIN

MING-MING

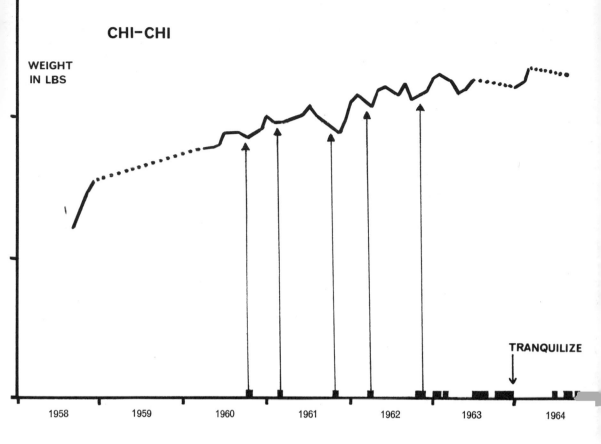

CHI-CHI

WEIGHT
IN LBS

TRANQUILIZE

1958   1959   1960   1961   1962   1963   1964

Chi-Chi's growth curve and her periods of heat. (The black rectangles on the base-line indicate the heat periods. The arrows reveal the way these periods relate to dips in the weight curve)

OPPOSITE
Growth rates in young giant pandas

Growth is rapid for a young panda and after only twelve weeks Ming-Ming had multiplied his bulk by forty times, weighing 12 pounds and measuring 2 feet in length. Three weeks later, on 1st January, he tipped the scales at $15\frac{1}{2}$ pounds and was nearly $2\frac{1}{4}$ feet long. By the end of January he weighed 21 pounds. Lin-Lin showed approximately the same rate of growth, reaching the weight of 22 pounds by 19th February, when she was about $5\frac{1}{2}$ months old.

Blind and -toothless at birth, the infant pandas are cradled gently by the mother during the early weeks. Film of Li-Li holding Ming-Ming, recently released from Peking, shows her cuddling and handling the baby in a startlingly human manner. While sitting up with her back leaning against the corner of her zoo den, she hugs and fondles the young animal, holding it to her chest. It is not until it is between three and four months old that the baby is able to crawl.

161

Li-Li was apparently extremely co-operative with the zoo staff and permitted her offspring to be removed for weighing. Sometimes she positively welcomed visitors, but on other occasions, she turned her back on them, grasping Ming-Ming tightly to her body. Zoo officials noted that Ming-Ming "shrieks at anything that seems threatening and is responsive to sound. If we call out his name two metres away, he never fails to turn back and come to us".

We only have four scraps of evidence concerning the rate at which the teeth develop. Ming-Ming had "cut several teeth" by January 1964. Su-Lin cut his first tooth on 18th December 1936 and had sixteen milk teeth by 8th February 1937, London's Ming (not to be confused with Ming-Ming) was losing her milk teeth and already had two adult teeth when she had attained the weight of 100 pounds. By drawing charts and working out probable rates of growth it is possible to arrive at a tentative generalization on tooth growth rate. It would seem that the panda gets its first milk teeth at about the age of $2\frac{1}{2}$ months and has nearly half of them by four months. At approximately 14 months they are lost and replacement by the adult teeth begins. (We admit that this is based on slender evidence, but it is the best that can be done at the present time.) The adult panda has forty-two teeth, comprising (on each side) three upper and three lower incisors, one upper and one lower canine, four upper and four lower premolars, and two upper and three lower molars.

As with the bears, the young pandas start small and then grow at a furious rate. It is most unfortunate that we have no single growth rate curve that is really complete. Ming-Ming and Lin-Lin will eventually give us this, it is to be hoped, but in the meantime all we can do is to fit together the various partial curves taken from different specimens, to see if they will give us an overall picture. In our chart we have included all the weight figures available for young pandas and have plotted them against the dates on which they were obtained.

It seemed likely that if there is a definite breeding season for giant pandas, then all the lines should fit one another to make a reasonable curve. This did not, in fact, happen. Ming-Ming, Lin-Lin and Su-Lin fitted together reasonably well and several other specimens such as Pandora and Pao-Pei appeared to bunch with them, but Pan-dee, Pan-dah and London's Ming formed a separate group. If one extends this latter group's curve downwards, parallel with the first group, then it strikes a zero (birth) point somewhere around March to April. This suggests a bi-annual birth peak, with one batch of offspring appearing in the early spring and another in the autumn.

As before, it must be admitted that this suggestion is based on very slender evidence, and it is true that certain specimens, such as Pan, do not fit the picture at all well. But there is one vital piece of information, previously unpublished, that seems to bear it out. Ever since Chi-Chi arrived at London Zoo in 1958, Head Keeper Sam Morton has been keeping detailed records of her development and behaviour. By turning his panda diary into another chart, it was possible to show that Chi-Chi's periods of heat followed a characteristic bi-annual rhythm. As we mentioned in the last chapter, her first period came when she was $3\frac{1}{2}$ years old, in the autumn of 1960. Morton noted that from 1st to 10th October she was off her food for the first time, was bleating and calling and was leaving scent marks on her "territory". Her mood also changed and she became more affectionate towards her keepers, pushing her rear end up against their legs if they stood still. The phase passed but re-appeared again the following year, from 12th to 20th February. During this eight-day period she ate nothing but the most tender bamboo shoots. From 7th to 20th October the same thing occured. In 1962 the spring period of heat did not begin until 12th March but was much longer, lasting until 1st April. The bleating and calling was stronger and more insistent and her passion for her keepers more intense. In the autumn of 1962 a change was noticeable. She came into heat on 20th October, but instead of becoming more friendly, she was "rather spiteful this time . . . increasingly vocal, calling and bleating, and shows signs of really looking for a mate. . . She now shows signs of temper when she is approached. She does not wish to go into her sleeping den at night and it is with great reluctance that she does so".

It seems as if Chi-Chi, after several unsuccessful sexual seasons, was beginning to become dissatisfied with her environment. When no mate materialized in response to her calls and her scents, her reproductive system went into revolt. As if determined to attract a male at all costs, it began to work overtime. As the chart shows, 1963 saw two spring periods of heat and two in the autumn. In addition, they were more intense and more prolonged. Her spitefulness developed into a "wicked temper". Her wanderings through her paddock became more agitated and elaborate.

Towards the end of 1963, the situation became serious. Chi-Chi had been on heat for so long that she was beginning to lose weight. During the earlier, normal heat periods of one to two weeks, her no-food-during-sex rule had resulted in brief but marked dips in the curve of her weight chart, but these were never any cause for alarm. They were quickly rectified as soon as the sexual phase was over. But now, with a period of heat extending over two months and showing no signs of ending, something had to be done. As we have already mentioned, the veterinary department was called in and a course of tranquillizers was administered. Chi-Chi began to take a little food, Sam Morton having discovered that he could tempt her with a bar of chocolate. Throughout the first half of December the tranquillizers were continued. She had been on heat since the beginning of October, but now at last she showed signs of calming down. Bamboo came back on the menu, and then dates. By January 1964 she was completely back to normal and was putting on weight again.

During 1964 the spring heat was seriously delayed, as if the reproductive system had worn itself out with its great efforts in 1963. It did not, in fact, appear until the early summer, and was brief, lasting only from 10th to 17th June. In early August there was another mild sexual phase and then a more typical one in September. Happily this proved to be normal in length and intensity and was terminated naturally without any veterinary

Giant panda weight curves. Arrows to right of chart indicate maximum weights for nine captive adults. Figures following names give sex and age in years. (see page 166)

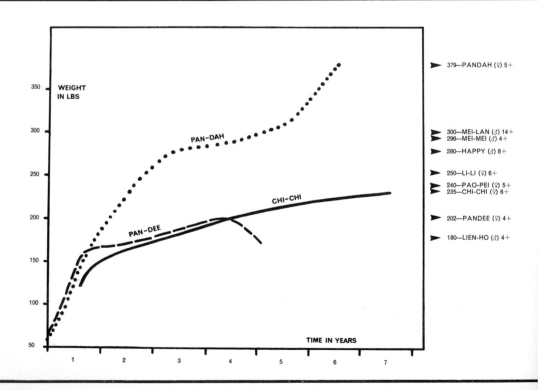

164

assistance. As we write these pages, in the spring of 1965, Chi-Chi is again enjoying a normal March-April sexual season and, for the moment at any rate, all is well once more. As to what will happen if she cannot be mated during the next few years, we cannot say.

Summing up Morton's records we can conclude that giant pandas probably have bi-annual periods of heat in the wild state, one around March and the other around October. Returning now to the question of possible birth peaks, it is obvious that the bi-annual heat periods would tend to produce bi-annual birth periods and this matches the rather scrappy information assembled in the growth chart. It looks as though pandas may mate in spring, in March, say, and then produce the offspring in September, or mate in October and give birth in April. This would give a gestation period of five to six months in each case.

Six months seems a long time to produce a 5-ounce baby, but there may well be some form of delayed implantation or delayed fertilization. In bears living in the Himalayas (and elsewhere, for that matter) the gestation period is seven to eight months, the young being conceived in the spring or early summer, but not born until the end of the year. A delaying mechanism is known to be operating there, and it may well also be active with giant pandas. On the other hand, we may have miscalculated badly and the true picture may be quite different. The facts we have to go on are so sketchy that all we have said on this subject must be taken as a purely tentative statement. (See postscript on page 209.)

One thing that we can be more certain about, however, is the age-weight relationship in young pandas. From the weight chart it can be calculated that:

5 ounces	0 months
7 pounds	2 months
20 pounds	5 months
60 pounds	10 months
80 pounds	12 months
120 pounds	16 months

This can be used as a rough guide for working out the age of any particular panda, where its early months were unrecorded. For example, Mei-Lan weighed 65 pounds when he arrived at Chicago Zoo and he lived there for a period of 13 years 10 months. This means that he must have been in the region of 14 years and 8 months when he died (which, incidentally, makes this the greatest recorded longevity for the giant panda).

Although Mei-Lan was the longest lived captive panda, he was not the heaviest. This record goes to New York's Pan-dah who at one point reached the massive figure of 379 pounds. It is difficult to decide whether this is a typical wild panda figure, or whether Pan-dah was grossly over-weight. The facts contradict one another. If one looks at Pan-dah's adult weight curve alongside those for Pan-dee and Chi-Chi, the big animal certainly seems to have a healthy enough curve. It almost appears as if the other two females became abnormally slowed down in their growth, just after passing the 150 pound mark. But if one then looks at the table of maximum recorded weights for nine of the adult captive pandas, it looks more as though it is Pan-dah who was abnormal. Certainly, the two longest-lived specimens, Mei-Lan and Pao-Pei, did not become so massive.

If one ignores Pan-dah, then the top three males bunch together at between 280 and 300 pounds, while the top three females group together at between 230 and 250 pounds. Until we have accumulated more detailed information, these are probably the best figures to take as the average weights for adult male and female giant pandas.

They are not, however, reliable enough yet to be of any value in attempting to sex an adult animal. As the history of captive pandas has already revealed, determining the sex of a member of this species at any age is an extremely difficult task. Of the fifteen giant pandas that have arrived alive in the western world, only ten have been correctly sexed. One in three have only been assigned their true gender after post-mortem. Su-Lin, Mei-Mei, Sung and Lien-Ho were all believed to be females, but proved later to be males. Pan-dee was thought to be a male, but was, in fact, a female. In addition to these, Chi-Chi was for a while held to be a male. As we have already explained, she arrived as a female, was then examined by a learned anatomist and declared masculine. Later, when she had to be sent to hospital for minor eye treatment it was discovered that, on closer examination, her original designation had been the correct one. Why is there such difficulty in this seemingly simple matter?

Many people imagine that all mammals show recognizable external differences in anatomy between the sexes, and that any expert can tell at a glance whether he is dealing with a male or a female. But this is far from true. In many species the sex organs are normally hidden and it is only during the mating act, when the penis is extruded, that it is possible to be certain. This is the case with the giant panda. There is no scrotum in the male and, to quote Dwight Davis, "in the subadult animal dissected (Su-Lin) the testes and their wrappings are so embedded in fat that they do not even produce a swelling in the contour of the body". Su-Lin was, of course, only 17 months old at death, but Royal Pocock was able to examine the adult London Pandas (Grandma, Sung and Tang) after death, and reported much the same state of affairs. He summed up the situation by commenting that "The testes are inguinal in position and there is nothing in the external appearance of the genital area to suggest their descent into a scrotum. The animal looks as if it had been castrated."

In 1941 Pocock published the first drawings of the male and female genital regions of the giant panda. The female details were taken from Grandma and the male from Sung (or possibly Tang). These were the only drawings available to assist with the sexing of Chi-Chi, and it was with Pocock's book in one hand that the anatomist entered the animal's enclosure in 1959. Peering back and forth between book and panda, he tried hard to make up his mind. Finally, he decided that Chi-Chi's genitalia matched up better with Pocock's masculine drawing and pronounced the animal male.

Chi-Chi was two years old at the time and had not yet started to exhibit sexual behaviour patterns. When this did occur, during the following years, it seemed once again as though she must be a female. She adopted the female copulation posture (lordosis) typical of many mammals, with her back arched down and her tail held high, and, as we have already mentioned, pushed her rear end up against the legs of her keepers.

Even at this point, however, one could not be certain, for sexually frustrated male mammals will often adopt "pseudo-female" sexual postures, just as frustrated females will sometimes mount. In a second attempt to clear up the mystery, efforts were made to obtain a close-up photograph of the genital region of the giant panda. It was argued that now she was sexually mature there would be a better chance of identifying the sexual anatomical details. A picture was obtained in the spring of 1962, when Chi-Chi was five years old. Photo-copies were also made of the Pocock drawings and the three documents were then shown to a number of experts, labelled only A, B, and C. A and B were the two drawings and C was the Chi-Chi photograph. The experts were asked to match C with either A or B. They were, in effect, being put in the same position as the anatomist who had entered the panda enclosure, except that they had a better view of Chi-Chi's genital region and, of course, it was now sexually mature. Despite this, opinion was divided and several authorities refused to

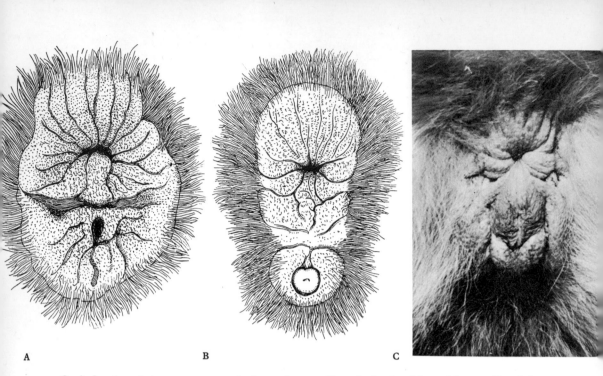

A   B   C

Genital region of giant panda. (Tail at top). A and B are the two drawings from Pocock. C is Chi-Chi. Does C match A or B? For answer see foot of page 170

commit themselves at all on the basis of the evidence offered them.

In order to put you, the reader, in the same position we are printing these three pictures together on this page with the same cryptic labels, A, B, and C. This will enable you too to enter the panda-sexing game. The correct answer is given at the foot of the next page, overleaf. In each of the three pictures the tail and therefore the anal region is at the top. The actual genital region is the lower area of naked skin.

In all three cases, one thing is clear; namely, that there is a large expanse of naked, glandular skin surrounding the ano-genital region. Pocock summarizes by saying that although this "skin is generally highly glandular . . . the pair of anal glands, normally developed in Carnivora, appears to be aborted as in bears. But no bear has a trace of the glandular area described". This tallies with observed behaviour differences between Chi-Chi and the various bear species. Chi-Chi frequently backs up to special rubbing points in her enclosure, arches her back, raises her tail and rubs her ano-genital skin region on to the hard surface. This deposits sticky glandular secretions and leaves a strong personal scent. It is a method of stamping the individual's identity on to its territory. Zoo bears have never been seen to do this. We shall have more to say about it later, but for the moment it is interesting to note simply that the ano-genital region has a triple rather than a dual function; it is not only concerned with defecation and copulation, but also with territorial behaviour.

In 1964, when Chi-Chi was seven years old she was, as already described, anaesthetized and examined in detail. More photographs were taken and one of these is reproduced on the next page. It shows clearly that the large *central* area of naked skin shown in photograph C does, in fact, open to reveal the female sexual orifice. This is, then, the vulvular region. This did not emerge clearly from the earlier photograph, and the *lower* area of naked skin had the appearance of a heart-shaped swelling similar to that drawn by Pocock for the male.

Unfortunately, Pocock's drawings exaggerated certain meaningless differences and concealed several meaningful ones. We now have a much more accurate drawing of the male genital region (of Su-Lin) published by Dwight Davis. For future reference it will be best to use this one and the later Chi-Chi photograph, rather than the earlier pictures.

There is some evidence that with older males the problem of sex determination may become easier. All the sexing problems have come with juveniles or young adults. Even "Grandma", who was described as an "old female", weighed only 170 pounds at death, and it is probable that she, Sung and Tang were, in reality, all young adults that had not yet reached full sexual maturity. Su-Lin, dissected by Davis, was also sub-adult, but he did examine an adult male as well (Mei-Lan) and makes the cryptic comment that "At sexual maturity the testicles are very evident." He does not enlarge on this point, or explain it. Ivor Montagu, when he visited the director of Peking Zoo, asked him how the Chinese zoo officials managed to sex their pandas. Tsui Chan-p'ing replied that it was very difficult indeed when the animals were young, but continued: "Only after about five or six years, with maturity, do the male's organs become visible." Having heard this, we then checked the ages of all the mis-sexed captive pandas (males that had been thought to be females until after death) and found that none of them had lived more than four years six months in captivity. Perhaps if they had survived longer their masculinity would have begun to reveal itself. Even so, this would not solve the problem of sexing younger pandas, and this is the time when it is most important to establish the gender correctly.

The Peking officials claim to be able to tell the sexes of their pandas by other secondary characters, informing Montagu that "The female is gentle, the male tends to be ill-tempered. The male is inclined to be moody and easily gets angry, the female is more sociable. The female is more handsome; her fur is better, finer, looks cleaner. The white on the back and even on the belly looks

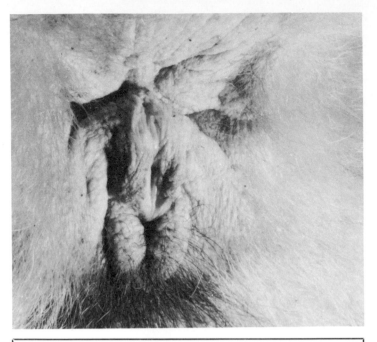

Later photograph of Chi-Chi's genital region, indicating female structure more clearly. (Zoological Society of London)

Recently published drawing of sub-adult male giant panda genital region. (After Dwight Davis)

Fig. 117. Perineal region of subadult male *Ailuropoda* (Su Lin).

Solution to panda sexing problem. A = female. B = male. Chi-Chi (C) should therefore be matched with A

whiter, The belly colour of the male is darker, there is more black." Asked specifically about differences in sexual behaviour, the Peking Zoo director replied: "if a male, the animal runs around all the time and will bark. The female will rub her lower parts on stone". Valuable as these comments are, it must be pointed out that Chi-Chi, a proven female, has been both "sociable" and "ill-tempered" at different times. Likewise, she has both run-and-barked and rubbed-on-stones when in sexual condition. (Also, the male Happy was seen to perform the rubbing action when at Leipzig Zoo). There may nevertheless be important differences in the *degree* to which the males and females perform these actions. Only when many more living specimens have been studied and compared, will we be able to say for certain.

In the meantime it is interesting to take a closer look at the way in which Chi-Chi behaves when she is at the peak of one of her periods of heat. To do this we made observations of her movements immediately after she was released into her paddock in the morning. At this point in the day, after being confined to her sleeping den all night, she is always at her most active. When she emerges she soon begins to clean herself, patrol her territory, and deposit her scent marks. Records taken on a typical heat-period morning present a clear picture of the sequence of events:

9th September 1964. Chi-Chi released into paddock from den at 09.26.

09.26: Chi-Chi calling out as she emerges from den door.

09.28: Walks over to log-pile, climbs up and stretches out.

09.38: Sits up on logs, scratches one side of face, then the other; then scratches flanks and feet. Sits up and raises her right back foot straight up so that she can rest her chin on it.

09.41: Scratches face again and gives full yawn. Scratches arms with back feet. Scratches tail with left back foot.

09.43: Scratches face with back foot and ear with front foot.

09.44: Leaves log-pile and walks back towards door of sleeping den.

09.45: Turns round, raises tail and presses ano-genital region against the concrete wall (A) just to the left of the sleeping den door. Rubs against wall with ano-genital region, depositing scent.

09.46: Walks to wall (B) on the other side of the cave entrance and scent-marks again. Rubbing action applied to wall eight times, during which the animal performs five vigorous head-shakes.

09.48: Sits up just behind logs and scratches again.

09.49: Moves over the keeper's door to paddock, sits up against wall by door and scratches again.

09.51: Returns to (B) and scent-marks again—three rubs this time.

09.53: Walks to the front of the pool, then turns sharply and goes back to pillar in middle of cave entrance. Scratches back against pillar.

09.54: Walks to (C) and turns, squatting, to place ano-genital region on slight ridge in concrete floor. Rubs on floor ten times. The fifth, sixth and seventh rubs are of lower intensity than the rest and during these three movements Chi-Chi again performs vigorous head-shaking.

09.55: Walks to tree-stump, sits down and scratches. Then sits holding top of stump with front feet.

09.56: Moves across to the pool and walks to water's edge. Front feet in the water.

09.57: Paws at water, "pulling" it towards her. Sits at water's edge. Slumps forward and stares fixedly at the reflection of her face in the water.

09.59: Walks back to wall (A) by den door and scent-marks there again, rubbing four times.

10.00: Starts patrolling territory again, walking right along the 75-foot front and back again.

10.01: Stops at drain (D) and deposits scent nearby, rubbing three times.

10.02: Walks right round the back of the enclosure and to the front again, where she sits down and rests.

Map of Chi-Chi's movements in her enclosure during observation period

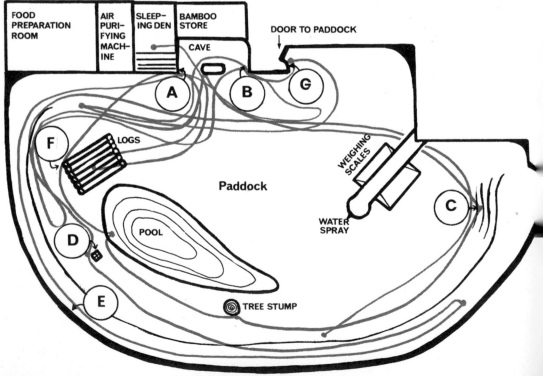

FOOD PREPARATION ROOM

AIR PURIFYING MACHINE

SLEEPING DEN

BAMBOO STORE

CAVE

DOOR TO PADDOCK

A   B   G

LOGS

F

Paddock

WEIGHING SCALES

POOL

D

WATER SPRAY

C

E

TREE STUMP

75 ft long

Public viewing area

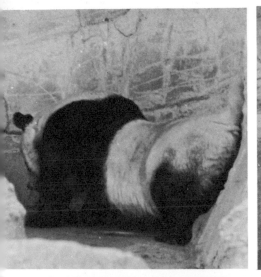

a. Chi-Chi in the scent-marking posture at point B (in the cave entrance).
b. Scent marking at point F (the log-pile). Note the "grin-face".
c. Scent-marking at point G. Note the humped shoulders and lowered back.
d. Circle shows glistening scent-deposit on wall. (Zoological Society of London)

10.03: Observation period ends. (Note: On other days, scent-markings were also seen at sites E, F and G on the map.)

The photographs showing these scent-marking actions clearly reveal the strange, high-shouldered posture, with the head held low and the back arched down. This is accompanied by slight movements of the back legs that rub the ano-genital region up and down over the wall or object being marked. The powerful head-shaking and head-tossing actions that appear during the rubbing sequence are associated with a special "grin-face", or an open-mouthed expression, and the whole performance gives the impression of a behaviour pattern of high intensity.

It could be argued that the animal is merely attempting to relieve an anal irritation, as domestic dogs will do, or that, in its frustration at being maleless it is trying to masturbate. In view of the fact that the rubbing actions are limited to several distinct sites in the territory, and that these same spots are used day after day and year after year, it seems more likely that the territorial scent-marking explanation is the correct one. Furthermore, although the rubbing actions occur with greatest frequency during the heat periods, they are by no means entirely absent during the rest of the year. Also, they are closely linked with territorial patrolling and appear rhythmically at certain times of day. Heavy scent deposits can, in fact, be seen at the points where the rubbings occur and the animal often sniffs at the spot before marking it. (Scrapings have been taken, but as yet await chemical analysis.)

The patrolling that takes place each morning is interspersed with cleaning actions, as the record shows. These are of no particular interest in themselves, except to indicate just how flexible the giant panda's body is. It is able to scratch its tail with its short back leg and can even, while sitting up, scratch the left back foot with the right back foot. Its reclining and resting postures are so varied and extraordinary that they give the animal an almost rubber-boned appearance. We have seen no other species that has thrust its back leg straight up in the air, whilst sitting down, and then rested its chin on it.

Chi-Chi at the water's edge. Giant pandas seldom enter the water and then only to paddle in the shallows. (Granada TV)

Scratching, with either front or back foot, and rubbing the back against hard surfaces, are the only cleaning patterns that appear with any frequency. Occasional licking may be seen and sometimes a front paw is used to clear some obstruction from the teeth, or to rub the eyes. Bathing is rare. Most pandas are reported as refusing to submerge themselves and there is no record of one swimming voluntarily. The most that they will do is to paddle at the water's edge, or play with water from a hose-pipe. A fine spray of water may be accepted on hot days and, if a block of ice is provided they will readily sprawl out on the cool surface.

Zoo pandas sleep sprawled on their bellies with all four legs spread out, or sitting up in a corner with their backs to the wall, or hanging in a fork of a tree, or lying flat on their backs. At night they seem to be more likely to adopt the last of these postures. From his studies of panda country in Szechuan, William Sheldon reported that "The favourite resting places of pandas are at the bottom of trees, under dead stumps, and in crevices of ledges. Dens under overhanging rocks in the midst of a precipitous slope of bamboos were often seen. Bamboo stalks had been broken and arranged to form a nest, and old piles of droppings gave evidence of frequent use. The natives say that it is in such places that the mother brings forth her young. I saw one instance of a well-used panda bed on the top of a large flat stump in an opening of the bamboo forests."

Like many mammals, the giant panda appears to be neither diurnal nor nocturnal, but crepuscular; that is, it becomes active in the mornings and again in the evenings, with a sleeping or resting period in the middle of the day and again in the middle of the night. Juvenile pandas are much more active throughout the day than adults and, as we have already seen, this can lead to disappointments for zoo visitors after a playful young panda has matured into a drowsy adult.

Locomotion in giant pandas is very similar to that in bears. There is the same "diagonal walk", to give it its technical name, and, at higher speeds, a clumsy trot. Unlike bears they have not yet been seen to gallop and hunters have several times commented upon the panda's apparent inability to flee at high speed. Sheldon reported that "On one occasion at a distance of 350 yards I observed two individuals on the edge of a bamboo jungle. Driven out by four dogs and warned by several high-powered bullets whistling about them, neither animal even broke into a run. The gait was a determined and leisurely walk. Again, Dean Sage and I observed another panda pursued by four dogs. In this instance he

*Chi-Chi standing
bi-pedally during play.
(Granada TV)*
RIGHT:
*Red panda standing
bi-pedally, with the help
of its tail. (Fox Photos)*

walked to within eight feet of Dean and was stopped only by bullets . . . During the course of tracking different animals for several miles I never saw a sign of one travelling faster than a walk."

Sheldon concludes from all this that "the panda is an extremely stupid beast". Whether, in fact, his observations reveal panda stupidity, or whether they indicate that the animal's heavy-boned body is incapable of really rapid fleeing, or alternatively that the species is simply not attuned to being hunted and has no panic responses with which to respond to the situation, it is hard to say. All that we can be sure of is that pandas are basically slow-movers.

Once seen, the giant panda's wiggling, pigeon-toed walk is never forgotten. Dwight Davis describes it with great clarity in the following words: "The head is carried well below the shoulder line, and the tail is closely appressed against the body. The stride is considerably longer than in bears, and as a result the gait is more rolling, with much more lateral rotation of the shoulders and hips than in *Ursus*. This gives a pronounced waddling character to the locomotion. The heavy head is swayed from side to side."

Pandas often heave themselves up into a standing position against a vertical wall, and sometimes do so in space, away from a vertical surface, but they have never been seen to walk bipedally like certain bears. They are also less efficient than bears at climbing. Young pandas will frequently clamber up branches and adults occasionally do so, but their tree-borne actions are extremely clumsy. Against a vertical, or almost vertical, tree-trunk, they will climb in a special way, embracing the wood and progressing by a series of caterpillar movements. When descending they usually come down backwards, tail-first, unless the branch is so near to the horizontal that they can actually walk down.

Despite their awkwardness in the trees, we know from the trappers' tales that giant pandas will take refuge aloft when pursued by dogs. No doubt if the dogs were unaccompanied by human beings the manoeuvre would work. After a while the pack would loose patience and follow up some new scent. This brings up the whole question of the natural enemies of the panda. Is the species really predator-free or does it have certain killers to fear? The evidence is conflicting. According to the director of Peking Zoo, "it suffers from the depredations of beasts of prey", but what could these be? There are only four other large carnivores in panda country: the Himalayan, or Asiatic black bear (*Selenarctos thibetanus*), the local race of the brown bear (*Ursus arctos*) known as the Tibetan blue bear, the Asiatic wild dog (*Cuon alpinus*), and the Leopard (*Panthera pardus*). The two bears might contest certain territories with the panda, but are never likely to act as panda predators. This leaves only the wild dogs and the leopards (and possibly some of the largest birds of prey). None of these, however, seems to be a very strong candidate as a panda-killer. Donald Carter sums it up by saying "In the dark recesses of the bamboo the animal has few foes except man. Leopards, wild dogs, or a bird of prey might take an occasional young one, but the old animal has little to fear." We are inclined to agree with this view, but it is worth quoting briefly from Hugo Weigold who, when discussing the panda tracks through the bamboo forest, points out that the thickets "often are compacted by the winter's snows, so that the trails followed run tunnel-like through them and vary in height from one and a half to five metres. They are used by other large mammals as well, the black bear, leopard, takin and wild pigs". He goes on to say that the native method of hunting pandas is "to set dogs on a fresh trail, and then to follow as fast as possible, without a halt, until the animal is overtaken and a shot obtained". If leopards are using the panda trails and if human beings can successfully pursue pandas along the same trails with dogs, then it would seem that the giant panda could easily be over-taken by the leopards as well.

The evidence is therefore contradictory. On the one hand, it is hard to believe that a giant panda, even an adult one 5 feet long, would offer much of a hunting challenge to a hungry leopard or a pack of starving wild dogs. On the other hand, it is equally diffi-cult to see how the panda could have survived at all if these lethal cats and dogs were a serious threat. As we have already heard, the giant panda is a slow-moving, clumsy, and not over-intelligent beast. It is unthinkable that such a cumbersome crea-ture should have persisted to the present time if there were any serious predator pressures working against it. Perhaps in some way which we do not at the moment understand, the animal's environ-ment protects it from its potential enemies. Perhaps the leopards and the wild dogs prefer not to hunt in the bamboo forest for some reason? Once again, we must await future field studies to give us the answer.

There is one other possibility that is worth examining. Although it would not appear at first sight to be capable of defending itself against a hungry "professional" animal killer, the giant panda is nevertheless able to inflict serious wounds if given the chance. Sheldon recorded that the specimen shot by his expedition "hesitated long enough to growl savagely, turn about, and bite one dog through the foot". We have already mentioned the damage done by Chi-Chi to her keeper, and we have since learned that when the Chicago male Mei-Lan was adult he mauled one of his keepers so severely that the unfortunate man had to have his arm amputated. The actual methods of attack vary according to the intensity of the mood. When mildly aggressive, the giant panda swipes out with a front foot. When it really means business, it runs or thrusts itself at the enemy, grabs out with a front foot, pulls the victim towards itself and at the same time delivers a powerful bite. Jaws that can crush hard bamboo stems can ob-viously inflict serious damage, and it is just possible that this is the panda's "secret deterrent".

Could it be that the panda's answer to the problem lies not in its "un-huntable" qualities, but in its "un-killable" qualities once it has been cornered? Its teeth are so massive and its jaws so powerful that it is just feasible that at the end of a comparatively easy pursuit, the unhappy leopard or wild dog pack is faced with the threat of a bite so terrible that it is simply not worth the risk of pressing home the advantage. This would explain three things.

Could the giant panda's black and white markings be a warning device similar to those of this American skunk? (Granada TV)

First, it would clear up the problem of why the giant panda has not evolved a more rapid form of escape, when sharing the region with potential killers. Second, it would explain why the animals cornered by hunters' dogs did not even *try* to escape. Third, it would provide a reason for the extraordinary colour pattern of the species.

The usual explanation for the black and white markings is that they are cryptic in function and help the animal to conceal itself against its snowy background. To quote George Goodwin: "As the white-and-black animal moves across the snow where rocks crop out and the trees cast dark shadows, it is often lost against the background." Photographs of captive pandas taken in the snow tend to back this up, but it is doubtful if anyone has yet made serious observations of this camouflage phenomenon operating in the wild state. Hung-Shou Pen, one of the few men to see living giant pandas in the wild state, wrote that "they flashed before us in all their beauty". William Sheldon, well-travelled in panda country, has stressed that "Other animals with more natural enemies and living in exactly the same habitat are mostly dark in colour and of a uniform shade. . . It is doubtful, therefore, if the characteristic markings of the giant panda are protective."

To sum up, it seems possible that on certain occasions, at special times of the year, in dim lighting, on particular types of terrain, the black and white markings may act as camouflage. At all other times and places it will probably be dramatically conspicuous. We have only to look to the skunks for a similar state of affairs. These animals have a secret weapon—their anal stink glands—and they fear few enemies. As with the giant panda, their fur is boldly marked in black and white, and this acts not as a cryptic pattern, but as an advertisement, a warning of their horrible hidden powers. Like the giant panda, they are rather slow and clumsy and not given to rapid fleeing. If harassed, they jog along until the situation becomes too trying, when they turn on their foe and threaten him. If he ignores this, they squirt their foul-smelling, near-blinding liquid at his face and wander safely away. Like the panda, they are not heavily endowed with intelligence; they do not need to be.

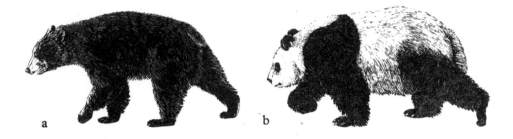

a   b

The more one thinks about it, the more the skunk-panda comparison fits. Pandas do not have anal stink-glands like the skunks (the ano-genital skin glands used in panda scent-marking are totally different), but if their secret weapon lies in the savage bite they can inflict with their broad jaws, then they would not require the additional aid of "chemical warfare".

The wild panda has often been referred to as "shy" or "timid", but a better description would be "retiring and elusive". Obviously this is not an animal that is going to go looking for trouble, but, on the other hand, when trouble finds it, it has shown remarkably little concern. Its behaviour in the face of human hunters could hardly be described as "timid". Furthermore, its zoo personality is one of serenity rather than anxiety.

By and large, then, it would seem that the famous black and white markings are most probably a warning pattern. It is interesting to contemplate how this situation could have evolved. If we think of the giant panda as developing from a creature rather like the red panda, then what are the evolutionary steps that would have been taken? If the proto-panda was—like the red panda today—a partial bamboo-feeder, it would only have been able to devour the smallest, tenderest shoots and the leaves. The more massive and heavier-jawed certain specimens became, the larger and larger would become their possible food stems. This would open up a bigger and bigger food supply in the bamboo forests. But, in order to be large enough to consume the heavier stems, the expanding panda would have to grow beyond a point where it could clamber nimbly to the safety of the tree-tops. The moment this ability had been lost, the (now medium-sized) panda would be in trouble. Still too small to defend itself against large killers, and too bulky to escape them, it would quickly die out.

This is apparently exactly what happened and explains why, today, we have only two members in the panda group—one small

d   e

The animals involved in the giant panda evolutionary controversy: a. bear. b. giant panda. c. red panda. d. cacomistle (primitive member of the raccoon family). e. raccoon. (After Dwight Davis)

and nimble and the other large and powerful. The middle-sized pandas that were intermediate between the two were no doubt a rapid failure and became extinct. Only those medium pandas that managed to evolved very quickly into the full-blown giant we know at the present time would have achieved any evolutionary success. Once a certain size had been attained, the already relatively vast crunching teeth would become effective weapons as well as bamboo-destroyers. Their development as feeding equipment would automatically make them secondarily available as defensive equipment as soon as they became absolutely, as well as relatively, huge.

At this point it would have become important to develop a warning coloration to fend off enemies at an early stage in an attack. Leaving it to the last minute to prove your superiority is a dangerous game. Even if you win, you may become damaged in the process. It is far better to have some kind of signal that operates at a safe distance. If the proto-panda was coloured like the present-day red panda, then very little change would be necessary. This small creature already has the black legs and the black marks around the eyes. The face is white and all that is necessary to convert it into a giant-panda-pattern is for the rust-red of the body to be replaced by white. (If one looks closely at a giant panda one can still see a faint yellowish tinge to the white, as if the process of bleaching was never quite perfected.) True, the marks around the eyes would have to be modified slightly and the dark hairs inside the ears would have to spread over their whole surface, but these are minor modifications. Assuming that the long tail, no longer needed for balancing, had been reduced to the giant's 5-inch white stump, and that the body proportions had become stumpier to support the heavier weight, then, hey presto, there was a giant panda.

Like almost everything connected with the giant panda, however, it is not as simple as this. The above story seems straightforward enough and, we must admit, we believe it to be true. But we must in fairness report that there is a school of thought which firmly states that the two living panda species are not closely related to one another at all. They contend that the similarities between them are entirely due to convergence and that they have only come to look alike and behave alike because they both inhabit the same part of the world and endure similar living conditions.

The arguments put forward for both sides are long and complex and we will only summarize them here. Nearly all previous authors have either strongly stressed one attitude or the other—often rather dogmatically—but we will do our best to summarize both points of view as objectively and fairly as we can, so that you, the reader, can decide which way you wish to vote.

Firstly, what exactly are the rival claims? The *raccoon school* insists that because the red panda is so obviously a member of the raccoon family (Procyonidae) and because the giant panda is so obviously a close relative of the red panda, then both the pandas must be placed together inside the raccoon family. This school of thought recognizes that there are certain important differences between the pandas and the other members of the raccoon family and so separates them into two sub-families within the family Procyonidae: pandas—sub-family Ailurinae; raccoons—sub-family Procyonidae. They do not think that the giant panda has any close relationship with the bears.

The *bear school* insists that the giant panda is a true bear and a member of the family Ursidae. They agree that the red panda is a member of the raccoon family and do not therefore believe that it has any close relationship with the giant panda.

Clearly this is no minor squabble over some trivial details. It is a basic argument about the very fundamentals of giant panda evolution. Is the animal really a bear-like panda, or is it a panda-like bear ? First, a brief look at the history of the controversy.

We have already described how Père David himself considered the animal to be a black-and-white bear in 1869. He did not appear to object, however, when Milne-Edwards, after studying its bones and teeth, decided it was closer to the lesser panda and the raccoons, and so in 1870 changed its name from *Ursus* to *Ailuropoda*. In the same year Gervais, on the other hand, examined its brain-case and claimed that it *was* a bear. He felt it was nevertheless sufficiently distinct to have a name of its own, and so placed it inside the Ursidae as *Pandarctos*. Later, in 1885, Mivart was forced to place the giant panda with the raccoon family because he found its similarities with the lesser panda inescapable. In 1891 Flower and Lydekker, in their work *Mammals Living and Extinct* reversed the process again and put the giant panda with the bears and the red panda with the raccoons. Winge, in 1895, decided that the giant panda was a bear, but that it belonged to a distinct group within the bear family and that its only close relative was the extinct *Hyenarctos*. In 1901 Lydekker made further skeletal studies and changed his previous view. Now both he and Lankester decided that the pandas belonged together in a special sub-family of the raccoon family. They put forward the two names mentioned earlier—Ailurinae and Procyoninae. They also changed the popular name of the animal from parti-coloured bear to great panda. In 1902 Beddard, in his *Mammalia*, put the giant panda back with the bears. In 1904, Weber in his work *Die Säugetiere* also placed it with the bears. In 1913 Bardenfleth studied the teeth in great detail and decided that their similarity with those of the red panda was due to convergence as a result of similar bamboo diets. He placed the giant panda with the bears. In 1921 Pocock solved the problem in a novel way by giving the giant panda *and* the red panda a distinct family apiece, thus completely begging the issue of their relationship. In 1936 Gregory and Raven examined the skull and viscera respectively and both concluded that the giant panda belonged with the raccoon family. In 1943 Segall studied the bony auditory region of both pandas and felt that *both* should be associated with the bears. In 1945 Simpson, in his *Classification of the Mammals*, put the pandas into the raccoon family. In 1946 Mettler and Goss (like Gervais in 1870) studied the brain of the giant panda and came to the conclusion that "the configuration of the brain . . . is identical with that of the bear". In 1951 Ellerman and Morrison-Scott, in their comprehensive checklist of *Palaearctic and Indian Mammals*, placed both pandas inside the raccoon family. Colbert followed suit in 1955 when he published his *Evolution of the Vertebrates,* commenting that "modern studies suggest it is a large procyonid that has paralleled the bears". In 1956 Leone and Wiens made serological tests that "clearly indicate that the giant panda belongs in the family Ursidae". In 1964 Davis published his massive anatomical monograph on the giant panda and firmly asserted that "*Ailuropoda* is a bear and therefore belongs in the family Ursidae. This conclusion is not based on one or a few characters, but on a host of similarities, many of them subtle, throughout the anatomy".

This then is the impressive line-up of big names involved in the panda dispute. If you join the *raccoon school,* you find yourself in the company of Milne-Edwards, Mivart, Lankester, Lydekker, Gregory, Raven, Simpson, Ellerman, Morrison-Scott and Colbert. If you enlist with the *bear school* you are siding with Gervais, Flower, Winge, Beddard, Weber, Bardenfleth, Segall, Mettler, Goss, Leone, Wiens and Davis. Either way, you would belong to a powerful team. On the basis of their respective reputations alone, the choice would be a difficult one. We must take a closer look at the specific arguing points.

No-one would deny that *superficially* the giant panda looks very much like a bear. It is the same size and the same general shape. No member of the raccoon family approaches either the weight or the body proportions of the animal. But this is not a very convincing argument. There are many cases of animals that have come to look very similar to one another—at first glance—but which are totally unrelated. Convergent similarities of this sort are so common that not even the most ardent members of the *bear school* would use this as a serious debating point. It is necessary to examine detailed structures or patterns of behaviour to see if there are subtle as well as crude likenesses.

The massive teeth of the giant panda have been a hotly discussed area. Most authors have agreed that they resemble closely only those of the smaller red panda. We will not record all the technical points of the arguments, but simply reproduce photographs of the upper jaws of the two panda species and a bear. These speak for themselves, showing clearly that the pandas are remarkably close but that both differs strongly from the bear in this particular respect. *Bear school* supporters have tried to minimize this difficulty by stressing that both pandas have to chew tough bamboo and that therefore one would expect a strong convergence here. They emphasize that if one considers the cheek teeth as a single unit rather than as a set of separately determined

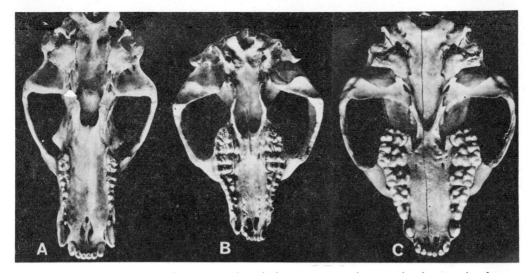

The teeth of a. polar bear. b. giant panda. c. red panda. (From Gregory)

characters, then it is easy to see how a simple genetic change could influence this whole area to produce a kind of dental gigantism. This would not, they argue, involve a mass of minor lengthy changes during evolution, but just a brief, simple enlargement. The *raccoon school* contend, however, that the minute details of the jaw, tooth by tooth, are so different from those of the bears that true affinity must be ruled out.

The *raccoon school* also points out that the panda skull is much shorter in the muzzle, much broader and generally more massive than that of the bears. Their opponents counter that this is merely secondary, following in the wake of the heavy dental developments. If there are to be large teeth, then they must have a suitably swollen housing. If they are to be crunched together effectively, then they must be supplied with enormous muscle-power, and these muscles must have strong attachments, hence a denser, tougher skull. A similar attack is launched against the famous "sixth claw" on the front foot of the giant panda. This, it is stressed, is simply a very recent adaptation to bamboo-feeding and could have been developed from either a bear ancestor or a raccoon ancestor. The come-back here is that the red panda uses a very similar grip when holding bamboo stems and has the necessary behaviour to provide the starting point for the evolution of a specialized structure like the "sixth claw".

The general nature of the giant panda skeleton has been held to be unbear-like in many detailed ways. It is said to give the impression of being the skeleton of a "fake" bear. This is especially true of the way the limb bones relate to one another. Also there is a generally heavy-boned quality about the panda skeleton. These differences are belittled by the simple device of claiming that, when the animal had to get a heavier head in connection with its feeding habits, it did so by getting a heavier skeletal system in general. Hence, the body passively became more heavy-boned along with the skull and the teeth, even though there was no need for this. It is admitted that the weighty body structure is a hindrance to the panda, but it is felt that, in the predator free world of the bamboo jungles this did not matter. If it slowed the beast down, this would not reduce its chances of survival. This is a strange argument, and it certainly seems more reasonable to assume that the giant panda was instead a rapidly enlarged red panda, if one wants to give a plausible explanation of these skeletal features. The point to remember here is that if the giant panda evolved from a bear, then its ancestor did not have to become generally enlarged, only more heavy-headed. As the bears had already evolved an efficient high-speed body, it seems odd that they should have thrown this advantage away. If, on the other hand, the ancestor was a small creature like the red panda, it would have to undergo considerable and rapid enlargement to become a giant panda. The new giant might well be of a clumsy design to start with. Polishing up of the final product of this evolutionary step would take some time. We would expect to have to wait a while to see the body clumsiness swept away. On this basis

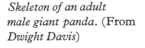

Skeleton of an adult male giant panda. (From Dwight Davis)

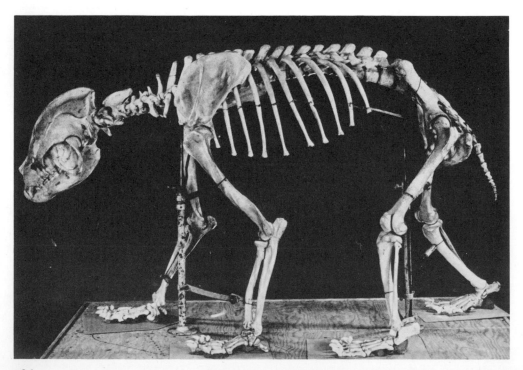

we feel that the giant panda has more the character of an old time bamboo-eater newly giantized, rather than an old time giant recently bamboozled.

Turning to the alimentary system, the fact that the small intestine is shorter and less complex than that of the bears is very difficult to explain if they are closely related. As even the hardened members of the *bear school* have to admit, one would expect the bear gut to become lengthened if the degree of herbivory were drastically increased. On the other hand, if the entrails were evolving rapidly from those of a much smaller creature, inefficiencies of the kind already referred to would be less surprising. Also the structure of the stomach, the liver, and various other alimentary characters are extremely similar to those of the red panda. These similarities do not appear to be simply the result of bamboo digestion.

In other body systems, such as musculature and respiration, there are striking similarities in detail between the bears and the giant panda. The meticulous dissections of Dwight Davis leave no doubt about this. But these systems do not differ so drastically from carnivore to carnivore and if any two species came to be about the same size and general shape, it seems likely that these systems would also come to resemble one another to a remarkable degree.

The S-shaped penis of the giant panda. (After Dwight Davis)

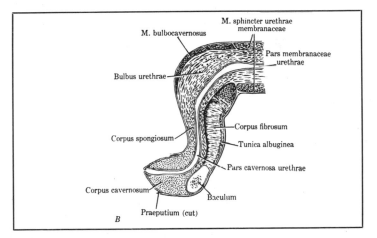

In one particular body system there are, however, some startling differences between bears and pandas. This is the genital system, where we find sex organs so astonishingly different that it really is impossible to accept them as having a recent common origin. A bear has a long, straight, tapering, pointed penis that is directed forwards. It is not dissimilar in design to the penis of a dog. The penis of the giant panda, by contrast, is ridiculously short for so large an animal, being less than three inches long in the adult. It is

187

cylindrical, S-shaped and posteriorly directed. It is very similar to that of the red panda. This likeness is extremely difficult to explain if the two species are not closely related, especially as the structure is so unique in its design. Dwight Davis, a staunch member of the *bear school*, found this very difficult to explain, but suggested that perhaps there had been a freak matching of two cases of arrested genital development. It was as if both pandas had become stuck almost at the embryonic stage in this particular respect. Davis comments non-commitally that "The significance of this convergent 'fetalization' of the external genitalia in two remotely related forms is unknown." It might have been better to admit that, on the basis of this feature at least, the word "remotely" is unjustified.

We have already pointed out that the large area of naked skin in the ano-genital region of the giant panda is a character that distinguishes it sharply from the bears. Likewise, its scent-marking behaviour is totally un-bearlike. The production of minute offspring, on the other hand, is typically ursine and provides valuable ammunition for the *bear school*. In the case of bears, however, this character is intimately linked with the mother's habit of taking a long, deep winter's sleep—virtually a hibernation. As the panda is reputed to remain active throughout the winter months it is obvious that the whole question of the detailed life cycle involved needs further study. Until this has been carried out, the existence of a 5-ounce newborn must be noted down as an important bearlike property for the giant panda. It is more reasonable to assume, at our present stage of knowledge, that this character is a hangover from a bear past than from a raccoon cum red panda past.

The vocal efforts of the giant panda have not previously been employed as a taxonomic character, as far as we can ascertain. Barking and bleating have been mentioned, but no-one appears to have attempted a serious analysis of the sounds. Head Keeper Sam Morton of the London Zoo has had daily contact with raccoons, pandas and all species of bears for a number of years. When we asked him whether he thought that the giant panda was a bear, his immediate reaction was to comment that "It doesn't sound like a bear. Bears roar—the panda bleats. It's totally different in that way." He then went on to discuss other panda characters, some pro-bear ("it moves and sits like a bear"), some anti-bear, but it is interesting that his first thoughts were concerned with the animal's vocalizations. In view of this we felt it would be worthwhile including here some sound spectrograms made from recordings taken during Chi-Chi's intense period of sexual heat in

*The calls of the female giant panda when in heat.
(Sound spectrograms by D. B. Fry)* 1. Loud call.
2. Medium call. 3. Soft call. 4. Dog-like bark.
5. Medium double call.

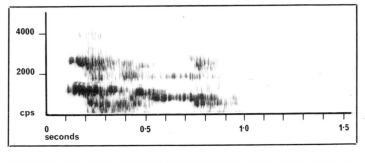

I

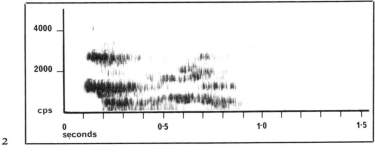

2

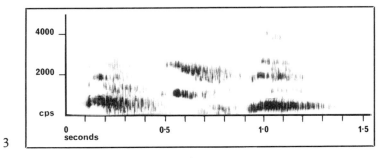

3

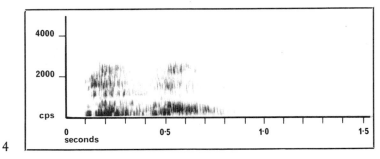

4

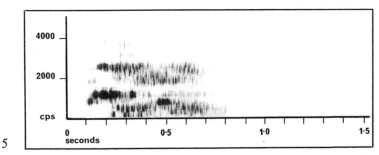

5

the autumn of 1963. She was so vocal at that time that it was only necessary to open the den door when she was inside her sleeping quarters and hold a microphone towards her to produce repeated loud calling. The cries came in various intensities and several of these have been included here. By themselves they cannot be of assistance to the panda ancestory debate, but when similar recordings become available for the red panda, the bears and the members of the raccoon family, it will be possible to carry out a detailed scrutiny of the different patterns and perhaps obtain some valuable relationship clues. In the meantime these sound spectrograph pictures provide us with a permanent and precise record of an important giant panda behaviour character, and we are very grateful to Professor D. B. Fry of the Department of Phonetics at University College London for preparing them and making them available to us.

The use of behaviour characters as aids to settling taxonomic disputes is a comparatively new trend. Until the last few decades anatomical features were all-important, but nowadays more and more categories of "species properties" are being brought into the front line. In addition to behaviour factors, there are also valuable clues to be gathered from such spheres as serological analysis and chromosome studies. In 1956 Charles Leone and Alvin Wiens of Kansas University published the results of a series of serological tests they had carried out using sixteen carnivore species, including the giant panda, the raccoon and the polar bear. The outcome was a serious set-back for the *raccoon school*. The figures showed clearly that "The serological affinities of the giant panda are with the bears rather than with the raccoons."

The method used was to inject serum from a particular carnivore into rabbits, where antibodies were produced. This provided a specific anti-serum against which the sera of other carnivore species could be tested. The strength of the reaction was held to indicate the "blood relationship" of the species concerned. The following table gives the results obtained with the three vital species. (The higher the figure, the closer the relationship is said to be.):

		SERUM		
		Giant Panda	Polar Bear	Raccoon
ANTI-SERUM	Giant Panda	100	80	22
	Polar Bear	76	100	41
	Raccoon	53	59	100

If these figures are reliable, then they are without doubt the strongest weapon in the armoury of the *bear school*. They are so important that the tests should be repeated as soon as further samples of the necessary sera are again available.

Against the serological results, the *raccoon school* can place recent chromosome studies by Professor William Davidson of the Department of Haematology at King's College Hospital Medical School, London. He reports that on the basis of chromosome numbers the giant panda (42) matches the raccoon (42), but not the bears (56 and 74). (He wishes us to point out, however, that until accurate chromosome counts have been obtained for *all* the bears, *all* the members of the raccoon family, and the red panda as well as the giant panda, any conclusions on this point must remain tentative.)

It seems as though at every step there is a strong pointer one way, followed straight away by something pulling in the opposite direction. We would like to be able to settle the matter for you with a final authoritative flourish, but clearly that is not possible. There is still a fascinating detective story here to be pursued in the years to come. Perhaps when the Chinese have been able to make lengthy studies of pandas, both in the field, the zoo and the laboratory, we shall finally know exactly what this strange creature really is. In the meantime, we can only gaze at it and make a guess. As we said earlier, we tend to side with the *raccoon school*, but we realize the position is a shaky one. We have been able to scrutinize living specimens of both species of pandas, all seven species of bears and six species of raccoons (the North American raccoon, the crab-eating raccoon, the coati, the kinkajou, the cacomistle and the olingo), over a period of years, and if we are forced to cast an intuitive vote it must be for the *raccoon school*. We cannot avoid a feeling that somehow the giant panda is a counterfeit bear rather than a true one.

Along with American palaeontologist Edwin Colbert, we imagine that the panda's evolutionary history went something like this: About thirty million years ago the ancestors of all the modern carnivores appeared on the scene. These were the miacids and they were small creatures rather like present-day civets. One development from the miacids was an elongated, short-legged, heavy-tailed creature called *Cynodictis*, the ancestor of all the dog-like carnivores. *Cynodictis* evolved in two directions. In one, it led to longer-legged animals that ran swiftly and became efficient, intelligent hunters. These are the dogs, wolves and foxes of today. The other branch led to the ancestoral raccoon, an animal called

Cynodictis, the ancestral canid. (From *Colbert*)

Phlaocyon, the ancestral raccoon. (From *Colbert*)

Phlaocyon. This appeared about fifteen million years ago and looked rather like the present-day cacomistle, and not too dissimilar from the red panda in general shape. *Phlaocyon* evolved in North America and from there it spread southwards to South America, where it evolved into such forms as the coati and kinkajou, and northwards, right across the land-bridge to Asia. This bridge, at present the Bering Straits, was an important passage joining the Old World to the New at that time, about ten million years ago. During the next few million years the ancestoral raccoons gave rise, in Asia, to the early pandas, small creatures rather like the present red panda. These spread across Asia to Europe and even as far as England.

Several million years ago one group of proto-pandas started to grow in size and rapidly developed into the giant panda. Both the lesser and the greater forms of panda were comparatively unsuccessful and their ranges became more and more reduced until today they survive only in their mountain retreats in central Asia.

While all this was going on, a separate line of proto-canid evolution was taking place. Some of the early dogs became heavier and heavier. Their bodies grew fat and bulky and their tails became shortened to blunt stumps. These massive proto-dogs evolved into what we today call bears.

This then is the picture—a raccoon branch and a dog branch, the former giving rise to the pandas as a splinter group and the latter the bears; each side, in other words, creating a heavyweight representative. Whether you accept this or not is up to you. We have presented you with the main arguing points and now you must decide how to cast your vote.

As a biological specimen, the giant panda is an enigmatic object, and we venture to guess it will remain so for some time to come. We can do no better than to close this part of the panda story with a quotation from Edwin Colbert: "So the question has stood for many years, with the bear proponents and the raccoon adherents and the middle-of-the-road group advancing their several arguments with the clearest of logic, while in the meantime the giant panda lives serenely in the mountains of Szechuan with never a thought about the zoological controversies he is causing by just being himself."

the appeal of
the panda

中国人民邮政

the appeal of the panda

CHAPTER NINE

*The first of the many ...
panda dolls in front of
Su-Lin's cage. (Chicago
Zoological Society)*

IF THE ZOOLOGISTS are uncertain about the true nature of the giant panda, the toy-makers have no such doubts. To them the animal is a super teddy-bear, a gift from nature to their bank accounts. Right from the start of the panda craze, commercialization of this new animal image has raced ahead. Giant pandas have appeared as dolls, hats, swim-suits and puppets. They have been used as motifs on postage stamps, wallpaper, tie-pins, brooches, cigarette packets and nursery furniture. There have sprung up panda postcards, songs, poems, books, films, strip-cartoons and TV shows. There has even been a panda cocktail: $\frac{1}{4}$ plum brandy, $\frac{1}{4}$ apple brandy, $\frac{1}{4}$ gin, $\frac{1}{4}$ orange juice. As symbols they have appeared in varying degrees of stylization on behalf of the World

A panda hat, London, 1939

A panda bathing suit, London, 1939

Punda cigarettes from Communist China

Panda postage stamp from Communist China

The menu card of the Chi-Chi Chinese Restaurant in London's Queensway

中华人民共和国
北京动物园
CABLE-PEKING 8537

PEOPLE'S REPUBLIC OF CHINA

PEKING ZOOLOGICAL GARDEN

196

a

HEINI DEMMER

BIG GAME CATCHING AND FILMING SAFARIS

WIEN, Austria
III, Hintere Zollamtstraße 17
Tel. 725151
Fernschr. 01 1729

NAIROBI
P. O. Box 30

Wien,
Nairobi,

b

25. BAND   HEFT 6   1961

DER ZOOLOGISCHE GARTEN

c

Help to save the World's Wildlife

Your contribution will help to save the world's wildlife and wild places

Send it now to:
World Wildlife Fund
2 Caxton Street
London SW1

e

Giant Panda emblems: a. Peking Zoo. b. Heini Demmer. c. Zoologische Garten. d. International Zoo News. e. World Wildlife Fund.

d

Wildlife Fund, the Peking Zoo, Zoologische Garten, International Zoo News, and Heini Demmer.

Despite the fact that only fifteen living specimens have been seen by the western world, the giant panda nevertheless manages to hold a place amongst the "top ten" animal favourites. In 1961 we prepared a competition for transmission on children's television, in which viewers were asked three questions: 1. Which animal do you like most? 2. Which animal do you dislike most? 3. Which animal topic would you most like to see dealt with in future animal programmes on television? They were told that prizes would be given only in relation to the third question, but that they would have to answer the first two to qualify. This was done to prevent any "clever" answers to the first two questions. The competition was transmitted in April 1961 and from the huge sacks of mail that resulted we selected a random sample of 4,200 cards. The sample was made up of 2,100 entries from girls and the same number from boys. With each sex, 100 cards were taken from each age group from four to fourteen inclusive. This made it possible to analyse sex and age differences in the various animal loves and hates. (Further details of this competition have been given in an earlier volume in this series—*Men and Snakes*.)

In the overall popularity figures, the giant panda came fifth, narrowly beating the bear. Approximately 8 per cent of all children voted for the panda as their top favourite, as compared with roughly 7 per cent for the bear. This put the panda ahead of such famous zoo stars as the elephants and the lions.

When the figures were analysed age-group by age-group, the giant panda was revealed as the special favourite of the very young. The 10 per cent level was exceeded only in the five-year-old group, and throughout the age range covered by the competition there was a steady falling-off in panda popularity. By the age of fourteen, the figures had sunk to the 5 per cent level. This follows much the same course as with the bears, but the decline is rather steeper with the panda figures. It contrasts strongly with the age changes in certain other "top ten" animals. Bushbabies and dogs, for instance, show a steady increase in popularity from four to fourteen, while horses rise to a peak of adoration at age ten and then begin to decline. It agrees best with the curves for the real giants of the animal kingdom, the elephants and the giraffes. These, like the giant panda, appear to have the strongest appeal for the very young children.

In general it seems that there are two basic phases of "animal-reactivity" in children between the ages of four and fourteen. The younger group (four to eight) react most strongly to big animals, while the older group (nine to fourteen) are more responsive to smaller creatures. This applies to both animal loves and animal hates. We have suggested that this indicates that there are two distinct types of animal symbolizing at work in the minds of children. The younger child appears to see animals as parent-figures, whereas the older child looks upon them as infant-figures. The younger child has not yet rebelled and prefers animals that can fit the role of the omnipotent parent. The older child, how-ever, is beginning to compete with its parents and at first does so by imitating them: *they* have been caring for it, therefore *it* will care for small animals. The pet becomes the infant-substitute.

The giant panda, by virtue of its very name, is clearly an ideal parent image. It appears to be cuddly and friendly and is therefore a good parent, as opposed to the gorilla which looks so fierce that it finds itself in the top ten animal hates in the role of *pere terrible*. It is interesting that unlike so many animal images the giant panda is sexless to a child. Gorillas are essentially male figures, regardless of their true sex, but pandas can be either or neither. This is reflected in the fact that almost exactly equal numbers of boys and girls voted for the panda as their top animal love. With nearly all the other animal "favourites" there was a marked difference in the figures for boys and girls. It is unlikely that this feature of the panda's symbolic nature is due to the fact that zoologists have also found the animal's sexual status rather con-fusing from time to time. Symbolic properties are not usually acquired in this way. It is more reasonable to assume that the panda is doubly difficult to sex—both in its external anatomy and its anthropomorphic personality.

Amongst adult panda fans, the appeal of the animal is complex, but undoubtedly includes certain child substitute elements, and it is important to realize that this is not precluded by the young child's view of the creature as a parent-figure. Symbolically and anthropomorphically, we all see animals in the way we want to see them, and this may differ drastically according to our age or sex. It is naive to imagine that any particular animal is a symbol simply of one single property or quality. Rhinos and gorillas, for example, are in the top ten animal hates for children, because they are "big, and vicious". But elderly people find them tragic rather than savage, because, like themselves, they are in danger of becoming extinct. In other words, when we go to the zoo we take with us our worries and our joys, our heroes and our villains, and we dole them out to the various species, casting each one in the role it is best equipped for on the basis of its accidental human resemblances. Obviously the giant panda must have extremely potent symbolic appeal to have raised it into the top flights of animal popularity on such a slender acquaintance. Somehow, it must have a multiple attraction to sell itself so well to such a vast audience. In order to see how this can have happened, we will attempt to dissect the species, not anatomically, but anthropomorphically. There seem to us to be twenty basic points in its favour, and they are as follows:

1. It has a flat face. The human face is flattened, compared with most animals, and any species that resemble man in this way are at an advantage. Walt Disney has always made use of this fact when creating animal heroes. They are given exaggeratedly flattened faces, whereas the animal villains are given dramatically elongated snouts.

2. It appears to have large eyes. Big eyes give an animal an innocent, child-like quality. Giant pandas do not in fact have large eyes, but the black eye-patches nevertheless convey this impression.

3. It has little or no tail. Human beings are tail-less and any species showing a similar condition, or having a short, inconspicuous tail are at an advantage.

4. It sits up vertically. Man is an upright species and any creature that regularly assumes the vertical position scores strong points anthropomorphically. Penguins, for instance, are the most vertical of birds and they are also the most popular. Dogs, so popular on other counts, lose on this one, and it has been necessary for man to train them to sit up and beg. (He has also flattened their faces by selective breeding and docked their tails.)

5. It can manipulate small objects. The famous sixth "claw" of the giant panda gives it a unique anthropomorphic advantage over other species. To be able to sit up and carry small food objects up to its mouth gives it very human qualities indeed. Amongst birds, the parrots are particularly good at this. They can balance on one leg, while the other is brought right up to the mouth for feeding. It is not surprising that of all birds they come second in popularity (next to the penguins). Most creatures have to lower the head to the food, and this puts them at a disadvantage in this particular respect.

6. It is a killer turned non-killer. Many carnivores are beautiful and popular animals, but they lose points because in order to survive they have to kill their prey. The lion creates a difficult problem in this respect. He is such a beautiful and dignified

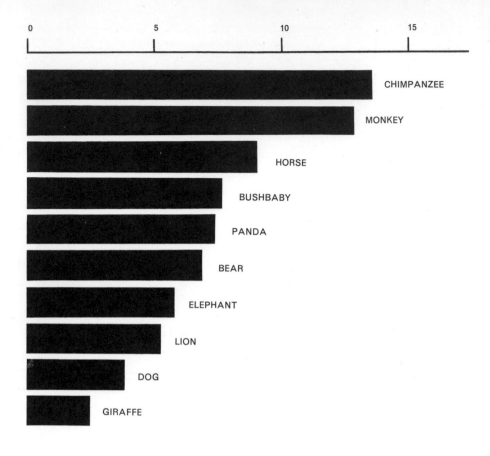

0　　　　　5　　　　　10　　　　　15

CHIMPANZEE

MONKEY

HORSE

BUSHBABY

PANDA

BEAR

ELEPHANT

LION

DOG

GIRAFFE

Top ten animal favourites. Shown as percentages based on answers from 4,200 children aged from four to fourteen

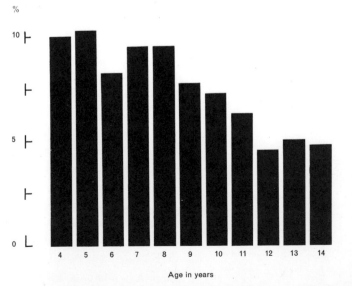

%

10

5

0

4　5　6　7　8　9　10　11　12　13　14

Age in years

Changes in the degree to which pandas are liked with increasing age. Based on answers from 4,200 children

200

creature that he gets into the top ten loves, but he also attacks charming little antelopes and gazelles, with the result that he also gets into the top ten hates. He is the only animal to find a place in both charts. The ambivalence he causes is not present in the case of the giant panda. Here is a species that is not only predominantly vegetarian, but has actually evolved from flesh-eating ancestors. Symbolically, he has seen the light and mended the wicked ways of his ancient predecessors.

7. It is harmless and friendly towards human beings. If an animal looks attractive and helpless, but is proved to be secretly rather aggressive and dangerous, then it loses points. Young and half-grown pandas are quite prepared to permit a great deal of mauling and handling without losing control. It is true that adults have occasionally bitten their keepers, but even so there are far more photographs of people petting pandas than there are of people petting other large carnivores.

8. It is sexless. As we have already pointed out, the giant panda lacks any external anatomical features that are obviously sexual. Monkeys and apes often have highly obtrusive sexual structures, both in the males and the females. These features often embarrass the human eye and work against the animals' popularity. Human beings keep their sex organs carefully covered; so does the giant panda.

9. It is playful. Human beings play a great deal. So do pandas, given a tyre, or a hose-pipe, or a step-ladder, a giant panda will quickly invent a whole series of gymnastics, just like a human child. Many animals never play and this works against them.

10. It is clumsy. When playing and also when going seriously about its business, its locomotion and general movements are cumbersome and clumsy. This gives it all the appeal of a small child that has not yet mastered its muscles. In the case of the giant panda, as we have already explained, it is due to the extremely heavy-boned nature of its skeleton.

11. It appears to be very soft. Babies are soft to their mother's touch and vice versa. Softness in animals is always appealing. To young children it spells mother and to mothers it spells baby. The mammals in general have won on this particular point. No birds, reptiles or fishes manage to get into the top ten loves. It is interesting that those few mammals that have donned hard shells, or armour, such as the rhinos, hippos, pangolins and armadillos, are often quoted as animal hates even though they are mammals.

12. Its outline is rounded. A rounded animal wins on the same principle as a soft one. Babies are rounded and the mother's breast is rounded. Again, it is interesting that mammals which are clearly soft, such as slender lorises or gazelles, but which are spindly and elongated rather than rounded, lose points. Heavy, curvaceous animals such as elephants and bears are more popular in general than slim and elegant ones.

13. It is black and white. Any powerful colour-contrast attracts human attention. The vivid coloration of the giant panda is immediately eye-catching. When domesticated species have lacked this quality, man has been forced to do something about it. Just as he has bred flat-faced dogs, so he has bred black and white dogs; also goats, sheep, cattle and almost any other domestic animal you care to mention.

14. It is a giant. The animal is not only big, which is a help in itself (because it brings it nearer to human proportions), but it is also specifically a giant. This means that it must be bigger than something related to it. Not simply a big animal then, but a *bigger* one. Men have always been fascinated by the biggest of anything, whether it is a fish or a female bosom. On this score the panda wins easily. Its nearest relative is only the size of a domestic cat.

15. It has an easy name. The word "panda" is pleasant to say. A child can mouth it at a very early age. Many animals have complicated names that work against their success. The delightful angwantibo, for instance, will never be a success, nor will the charming little sminthopsis. A short, simple and distinctive name is a great advantage.

16. It has an historical precursor. The teddy bear was already winning friends and influencing people before the living panda came on the scene. Much of the groundwork for this particular kind of animal shape had been done. When the giant panda arrived as a kind of super teddy bear, it was able to build on the reputation of its plain-coloured predecessor.

17. It is rare. Familiarity has never been able to breed contempt in the case of the giant panda. It has come on the scene suddenly, attended by all the hullabaloo and paraphernalia of a great star. There has always been the sense that this is *it*; this is the only time it will be possible to encounter one. After this one, perhaps never again will the extraordinary creature be available to gaze upon. It is not only rare in captivity, but also rare in the wild. One authority has claimed there are no more than forty-five in the whole world. Others have stated that there are only a few hundred. (We ourselves put the figure at several thousands.) This has given a sense of urgency to the presence of a living panda. One must look now, or it will be too late. It has also given rise to a protective

Fig. 73. An idea for a brown bear and a panda made from circles.

The evolution of the giant panda from the teddy bear—in the toy-makers' world. (From Hutchins)

feeling: we must help the creature to survive. It is clearly in trouble and therefore appealingly helpless. A biological victim to be nursed back to ecological health.

18. It comes from a remote and mysterious habitat. The almost impenetrable mountain forests where it makes its home are surrounded by mystery. This gives it an attractively romantic quality that a more home-grown species can never hope to acquire.

19. It has had a strange history of discovery. From the colourful French Priest, Père David, to the extraordinary Ruth Harkness and the tragic Tangier Smith, the panda has been served well by its human promoters. Other creatures have come into our sphere of knowledge in a vague and often rather mundane way, but the giant panda has burst upon us as a staggering prize or the goal of a fantastic quest.

20. It is immensely valuable. In terms of hard cash, a living panda is worth more than any other wild animal known to science today. Along with the other properties mentioned above, this adds considerably to the panda mystique.

With these twenty points in its favour the giant panda cannot, and does not, fail to capture the imagination of the world. It has so many appealing qualities that even if some of them disappear with the passage of time, it will still have enough left to ensure it a place amongst the really great animal stars. We only hope that in writing this book we shall have helped to keep the spotlight glowing even more brightly on this fascinating and delightful creature. It has had adoration a-plenty, but it deserves much more serious interest than it has received in the past. We still know shamefully little about its life in the wild and we are still unable to record many of the details of its natural behaviour. Until this can be done, there is a considerable danger that we may lose it forever from the face of the earth. It is in many ways a biological failure and it needs our help if it is to survive, but we cannot give this help until we know more about it. As China is at present refusing to release any know-ledge it may have acquired in recent years, and will not permit outsiders to visit the wild home of the panda, we must rely en-tirely on the Chinese zoologists themselves to investigate the situation and take whatever steps are necessary. Unfortunately, when westerners were able to visit western China and make con-tact with the panda, we were at the primitive stages of shooting or grabbing them. Now that we are more enlightened and would not dream of so much as touching one, we are banned from the locality. Requests to take film cameras to Szechuan and attempt to record the private life of the giant panda have encountered a bamboo wall even more impenetrable than the panda's own bamboo forest. But who can blame the Chinese authorities? They have learnt their lesson and now we must pay for the behaviour of our earlier representatives. All we can do is wait and hope that Chinese zoology will make strides big enough and fast enough to enable the world to salvage one of its most exotic and enigmatic natural treasures: *Ailuropoda melanoleuca*, the fabulous giant panda.

a concise history of pandas

1821 6th Nov.: Major General Thomas Hardwicke introduces the red panda to science in a paper read to the Linnean Society of London.

1825 June: Frédéric Cuvier publishes the first official description of the red panda, naming it *Ailurus fulgens*.

1827 Hardwicke's paper finally published, but concedes priority to Cuvier.

1869 11th Mar.: Père David discovers the giant panda. Sees skin for first time.

21st Mar.: Père David sends panda skin to Paris with brief description and request that it should be published. His wish is carried out in the journal of the Paris Natural History Museum. Animal named *Ursus melanoleucus*.

23rd Mar.: Young giant panda caught and killed and brought to Père David.

1st Apr.: Père David is given body of adult giant panda.

22nd May: First living red panda to reach Europe arrives at London.

1870 Alphonse Milne-Edwards decides the giant panda is not a bear and re-names it *Ailuropoda melanoleuca*.

1872 Père David publishes the first notes on the habits of the giant panda.

1874 Milne-Edwards publishes the first detailed anatomy of the giant panda.

1915 A. S. Woodward publishes details of a fossil giant panda from Burma, *Aelureidopus baconi*.

1916 Hugo Weigold of the Stoetzner Expedition acquires living young giant panda, which dies shortly after. Expedition collects total of six skins.

1923 W. D. Matthew and W. Granger publish details of a fossil giant panda from the Pliocene deposits of Eastern Szechuan, naming it *Aeluropus fovealis*.

1929 13th Apr.: Theodore and Kermit Roosevelt are first

westerners to shoot adult giant panda, at Yehli in Sikang Province, during the Kelley-Roosevelt Expedition. Later publish a book *Trailing the Giant Panda*.

1931   13th May: Ernst Schaefer shoots a young female giant panda on the Brooke Dolan Expedition.

1934   8th Dec.:   Dean Sage and William Sheldon shoot an old female giant panda on the Dean Sage Expedition.

1935   April: Capt. H. C. Brocklehurst shoots giant panda.

1936   9th Nov.:   Mrs. Ruth Harkness acquires living young giant panda, Su-Lin, thought to be female.

18th Dec.:   Su-Lin arrives in San Francisco, being first living giant panda to reach the West.

23rd Dec.:   Su-Lin arrives in New York.

1937   8th Feb.:   Su-Lin deposited at Brookfield Zoo, Chicago.

April: Su-Lin acquired by Brookfield Zoo, thus becoming first zoo-owned giant panda.

Autumn: Back in China, Ruth Harkness finds two more young pandas, believing both to be females. Arranges to bring one to U.S.A. as mate for Su-Lin.

1938   Ruth Harkness publishes her book *The Lady and the Panda*.

18th Feb.:   Ruth Harkness arrives at Brookfield Zoo with second living panda, Diana, later re-named Mei-Mei.

1st Apr.:   Su-Lin dies from food obstruction. Post-mortem reveals it was a male. Ruth Harkness leaves for third trip to China to obtain mate for Mei-Mei.

10th Jun.:   Roy Spooner brings young female giant panda, Pandora, to New York Zoo.

24th Dec.:   Floyd Tangier Smith arrives in London with five giant pandas: young female called Ming and four adults: Grumpy, Dopey, Happy and Grandma. Grumpy and Dopey re-named Tang and Sung, thought to be male and female; Happy, a male, and Grandma, an old female. Sixth panda said to have died on the voyage.

1939   9th Jan.:   Grandma dies of pneumonia.

26th Jan.:   Happy sold to Germany and tours German zoos.

	1st May:	Male Pan arrives at New York zoo as mate for Pandora.
	23rd May:	Sung transferred to Whipsnade Park.
	24th May:	Happy arrives in France, stays at Vincennes Zoo in Paris.
	24th Jun.:	Happy arrives at St Louis Zoo, which becomes his permanent home.
	1st Sep.:	Ming and Tang evacuated from London to Whipsnade two days before war declared.
	12th Sep.:	St. Louis Zoo acquires female Pao-Pei as mate for Happy.
	16th Nov.:	Chicago Zoo acquires third panda, male Mei-Lan.
	18th Dec.:	Sung dies in London Zoo sanatorium. Post mortem reveals it was a male.
1940	14th Mar.:	Ming returns from Whipsnade to war-time London.
	23rd Apr.:	Male Tang dies.
	5th May.:	Male Pan dies.
	17th Oct.:	Ming returns to Whipsnade.
1941	13th May:	Female Pandora dies.
	30th Dec.:	John Tee-Van arrives at New York with Pan-dee and Pan-dah, thought to be a pair and presented to the American people by Madame Chiang Kai-Shek.
1942	7th Jul.:	Ming returns once again to war-time London from Whipsnade.
	3rd Aug.:	Mei-Mei dies at Chicago. Post mortem reveals it was a male.
	15th Oct.:	Ming returns to Whipsnade.
1943	3rd Jun.:	Ming returns to London Zoo for the last time.
1944	26th Dec.:	Ming dies.
1945	4th Oct.:	Pan-dee dies at New York. Post mortem reveals it was a female.
	31st Dec.:	Lien-Ho caught in Szechuan for London Zoo.
1946	10th Mar.:	Lien-Ho arrives in London. At this time also known by names Lien-Hop, Unity, and Union. Thought to be a female.
	11th May:	Happy dies at St. Louis.
1950	22nd Feb.:	Lien-Ho dies of pneumonia.
1951	31st Oct.:	Pan-dah dies at New York.
1952	24th Jun.:	Pao-Pei dies at St. Louis.
1953	5th Sep.:	Mei-Lan dies at Chicago.

1955		Peking Zoo acquires three young "female" giant pandas: Ping-Ping, Hsing-Hsing, and Chi-Chi (I). (Ping-Ping later shown to be male.)
1956		Peking acquires another female, Ssu-Mao and, in the autumn, an un-named male.
	31st Dec.:	Un-named male at Peking dies.
1957		Peking acquires a female, Li-Li.
	18th May:	Peking gives giant panda Ping-Ping to Moscow.
	Dec.:	Six month old cub is caught in Szechuan. It is a female called Chi-Chi (II).
1958	Jan.:	Chi-Chi (II) arrives in Peking.
	May:	Heini Demmer travels to Peking to obtain panda by exchange negotiation. Selects Chi-Chi (II) and takes her to Moscow, then Berlin, Frankfurt and Copenhagen.
	5th Sep.:	Chi-Chi arrives in London for three-week visit.
	26th Sep.:	Chi-Chi acquired by London Zoo. Director of Moscow Zoo visits pandas in Peking Zoo.
1959	18th Aug.:	Male An'-An' sent from Peking to Moscow. Male Pi-Pi caught and installed in "husbandry station".
1960	Oct.:	Chi-Chi comes into heat for the first time.
1961	29th May:	Ping-Ping dies in Moscow. Proves to be male.
	Apr.:	Ivor Montagu visits Peking Zoo, photographs female Li-Li in enclosure with un-named male. Ascertains that there are five other giant pandas in Chinese Zoos at Shanghai, Nanking, Kunming (Yunnan), and Shensu (Chengtu?).
1962		Li-Li's male replaced by Pi-Pi, from husbandry station.
1963	9th Sep.:	Li-Li gives birth to male Ming-Ming, the first captive born giant panda.
1964		Shanghai Zoo now known to have three giant pandas, Canton two, Chengtu three, and Pinkiang (Harbin) one. Ming-Ming is separated from parents.
	4th Sep.:	Li-Li gives birth to female Lin-Lin at Peking. Second giant panda born in captivity.
	7th Dec.:	D. Dwight Davis of Chicago publishes major monograph on the anatomy of the Giant Panda.
1965	15th Feb.:	Lin-Lin is separated from Li-Li.

ADDITION TO APPENDIX I

The text of Men and Pandas *was completed in the spring of* 1965.
Since that time certain new information has become available and,
although it is too late to include it in the main body of the text, it can
be summarized here as follows:

1965 Sep.:   Caroline Jarvis, editor of the *International Zoo
Yearbook,* visits Chinese zoos and ascertains
that Peking Zoo now has seven giant pandas:
Li-Li, Pi-Pi, Ming-Ming, Lin-Lin, and also a
young adult female and a pair of wild-caught
cubs under one year old. Shanghai Zoo has one
young male and two adult females. Nanking
has a female, Harbin a male, Hangchow a
female, and Pyongyang in North Korea a pair.
There are still three giant pandas (sex unknown) at Chengtu and an unknown number at
Chungking. Chinese provide accurate figures
for giant panda gestation period: Ming-Ming
148 days, Lin-Lin 120 days. Latter thought to
be premature (Lin-Lin had dead twin), so
giant panda gestation period therefore appears
to be five months. (See *Animals* magazine,
April 1966.)

1966 4th Feb.:   Curator of Mammals of London Zoo visits
Russia at invitation of Moscow Zoo to discuss
possibilities of mating An'-An' and Chi-Chi.
Moscow Zoo director, Igor Sosnovsky, agrees
to Chi-Chi visiting An'-An' in the spring and
states that, as the Russian interest in the project is purely scientific, the offspring, if any,
will belong to London. Information obtained
from Moscow Zoo indicates that male An'-An'
has two periods of sexual excitement each
year, a strong one from February to May and
a weaker one in the autumn. Like female Chi-
Chi he scent-marks, calls ("bleating like a
sheep"), and goes off his food during these
sexual phases. His weight is 339 pounds and
he has very obvious testicular swellings. The
highest weight recorded for the earlier Moscow
giant panda, Ping-Ping, was 399 pounds,

making it the largest known specimen to date. Neither of the Moscow pandas has had bamboo in their diet, which may account for their heavier weights. (See also Sosnovsky in *Priroda*, No. 4, 1958.)

1966 11th Mar.: Chi-Chi leaves London for Moscow in specially modified B.E.A. Vanguard aircraft accompanied by her head-keeper and London Zoo's senior veterinary officer.

26th Mar.: Chi-Chi and An'-An' meet one another through wire partition. They respond by barking and show much curiosity.

31st Mar.: Chi-Chi and An'-An' put together in enclosure but after circling and snarling they start to fight and have to be separated. (At the time of writing the mating project is still continuing.)

Zoological Society of London. (Photo: Lyster)

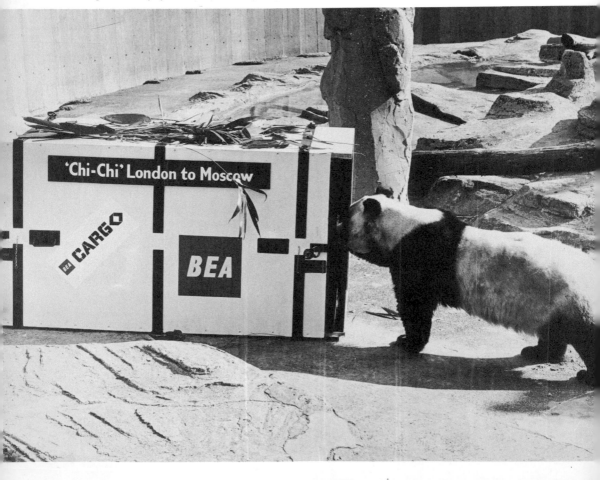

live pandas outside the orient—longevity chart

Name of panda	Sex of panda	Person involved	Final zoo home	Date of arrival at zoo	Date of death at zoo	Weight on arrival (lb.)	Life span in zoo (years/months)	Estimated age on arrival (months)	Estimated total longevity (years/months)
1. **Mei-Lan**	Male	A. T. Steele	Chicago	16 Nov. 39	5 Sep. 53	65	13/10	10	14/8
2. **Pao-Pei**	Female	G. Campbell	St. Louis	12 Sep. 39	24 Jun. 52	60	12/9	10	13/7
3. **Pan-dah**	Female	J. Tee-Van	New York	30 Dec. 41	31 Oct. 51	57	9/10	10	10/8
4. **Chi-Chi**	Female	H. Demmer	London	5 Sep. 58	(still living at 5 Apr. 66)	122	7/7	16	8/11+?
5. **Happy**	Male	F. Tangier Smith	St. Louis	24 Jun. 39	10 Mar. 46	240	6/9	24+?	8/9+?
6. **An'-An'**	Male	I. Sosnovsky	Moscow	18 Aug. 59	(still living at 5 Apr. 66)	231	6/8	24+?	8/8+?
7. **Ming**	Female	F. Tangier Smith	London	24 Dec. 38	26 Dec. 44	56	6/0	10	6/10
8. **Ping-Ping**	Male	I. Sosnovsky	Moscow	18 May 57	29 May 61	?	4/0	24+?	6/0+?
9. **Mei-Mei**	Male	R. Harkness	Chicago	18 Feb. 38	3 Aug. 42	50?	4/6	9?	5/3?
10. **Pan-dee**	Female	J. Tee-Van	New York	30 Dec. 41	4 Oct. 45	62	3/9	10	4/7
11. **Lien-Ho**	Male	Ma Teh	London	11 May 46	22 Feb. 50	40	3/9	7	4/4
12. **Pandora**	Female	R. C. Spooner	New York	10 Jun. 38	13 May 41	35	2/11	7	3/6
13. **Tang**	Male	F. Tangier Smith	London	24 Dec. 38	23 Apr. 40	150?	1/4	18?	2/10?
14. **Sung**	Male	F. Tangier Smith	London	24 Dec. 38	18 Dec. 39	150?	1/0	18?	2/6
15. **Pan**	Male	Den Wei-Han	New York	1 May 39	5 May 40	72	1/0	11	1/11
16. **Grandma**	Female	F. Tangier Smith	London	24 Dec. 38	9 Jan. 40	160?	0/1	19?	1/8
17. **Su-Lin**	Male	R. Harkness	Chicago	8 Feb. 37	1 Apr. 38	14	0/4	4	1/6

18 WING-WING Wash DC
19 HSING-HSING " "
20 ?
22 Paris
23 Paris

bamboos acceptable to the giant panda

APPENDIX III

The following types of bamboo are known to be palatable to the giant panda:

1. *Arundinaria tecta* Mulhb. Switch Cane. Native to the southern states of the U.S.A.

2. *Bambusa multiplex* (Lour.) Raeusch. Hedge Bamboo. Native to Kwangtung, China, and introduced in warm regions throughout the world as a hedge and potted ornamental.

3. *Dendrocalamus strictus* (Roxb.) Nees. Native to India.

4. *Sinobambusa tootsik* (Mak.) Makino. Native to China; introduced in the Hawaiian Islands and continental United States.

5. *Phyllostachys sp.* A Chinese bamboo in cultivation at Chengtu, Szechuan, China.

6. *Pseudosasa japonica* (S. & Z.) Mak. (=*Arundinaria japonica* S. & Z.) Metake. A Japanese bamboo widely disseminated in cultivation.

7. *Sasa senanensis* (Franch. & Sav.) Rehder. A large-leaved Japanese bamboo of low stature.

8. *Sasa chrysantha* (Mitf.) E. G. Camus. (=*Arundinaria chrysantha*). A small Japanese bamboo.

9. *Sinarundinaria sp.* Native to the haunts of the panda at altitudes between 6,000 and 9,000 feet in the mountains of Szechuan.

This list is based on a report by F. A. McClure of the Division of Plant Exploration and Introduction, Bureau of Plant Industry, U.S. Department of Agriculture, in Washington, D.C. Nos. 5 and 9 were brought back from China by Mr. Tee-Van when he collected Pan-dee and Pan-dah. No. 6 is the most common species of bamboo in cultivation in the colder regions of the world and is usually the mainstay of captive panda feeding. (It is also acceptable to the red panda, which in addition readily takes chopped fruits and vegetables such as oranges, bananas, apples and carrots.)

bibliography

Allen, G. M. (1938) *The Mammals of China and Mongolia*. Part I. Amer. Mus. Nat. Hist.

Anon. (1873) *Natural History of North China with notices of that of the South, West and North-East and Mongolia and Tibet, compiled chiefly from the travels of Père Armand David*. Da Costa and Co., Shanghai.

Anon. (1942) Panda up a tree. *Animal Kingdom*, 45, p. 79.

Anon. (1963) Focus on Chi-Chi. *Animals*, 1 (17), pp. 13–15.

Anon. (1964) Giant Panda bred in Peking Zoo. China Reconstructs, 13 (3), p. 27.

Anderson, J. (1869) Letter dated Indian Museum, Calcutta, 11th April 1869, to the secretary of the Zoological Society of London. Proc. Zool. Soc. London, pp. 278–279.

Bardenfleth, K. S. (1913) On the systematic position of *Aeluropus melanoleucus*. Mindeskr. Jaetus Steenstrup, art. 17, pp. 1–15.

Bartlett, A. D. (1870) Remarks on the habits of the Panda (*Aelurus fulgens*) in captivity. Proc. Zool. Soc. London, pp. 769–772.

Bartlett, A. D. (1900) *Wild Beasts in the Zoo*. Edited by Edward Bartlett, Chapman and Hall, London.

Bean, R. (1937) Giant Panda. Guide Book, Chicago Zool. Park, 1937.

Bean, R. (1948) Giant Panda. Guide Book, Chicago Zool. Park, 1948.

Bien, M. N. and L. P. Chia (1938) Cave and rock-shelter deposits in Yunnan. Bull. Geol. Soc. China Peking, 18, pp. 325–347.

Blair, W. R. (1938) Pandora in her new home. Bull. New York Zool. Soc., 41, pp. 119–122.

Brightwell, L. R. (1946) The Giant Panda, its history in ancient China and modern Europe. *Field*, 187, pp. 497–498.

Brightwell, L. R. (1952) *The Zoo Story*. Museum Press, London.

Brocklehurst, H. C. (1936) The Giant Panda. J. Soc. Preserv. Faun. Empire London, 28, pp. 21–23.

Burton, M. (1950) Some mammals discovered during the last century. *Ill. London News*, 217, pp. 28–31.

Carlsson, A. (1926) Ueber *Ailurus fulgens*. Acta Zool., 6, pp. 269–305.

Carter, T. D. (1937) The giant panda. Bull. New York Zool. Soc., 40, pp. 6–14.

Chaworth-Musters, J. L. (1946) The discoverer of the Giant Panda: Père Armand David, 1826–1900. *Zoo Life*, 1, pp. 70–71.

Chjan, Kh-Yu and L. Liu (1959) Anatomy of the digestive system of *Ailuropoda melanoleuca*. Acta Zool. Sinica 11, pp. 443–449.

Colbert, E. H. (1938) The panda; a study in emigration. Nat. Hist., 42, pp. 33–39.

Crandall, L. S. (1964) *The management of Wild Mammals in Captivity*. Univ. of Chicago Press, Chicago.

David, A. (1869) Voyage en Chine. Nouv. Arch. Mus. Hist. Nat. Paris, 5 (Bulletin), pp. 3–13.

David, A. (1872) Rapport adressé a MM. Les Professeurs-Administrateurs de Museum D'Histoire Naturelle. 15th December 1871. Nouv. Arch. Mus. Hist. Nat. Paris, 7 (Bulletin), pp. 75–100.

David, A. (1874) Journal d'un Voyage dans le centre de la Chine et dans le Thibet Oriental. Nouv. Arch. Mus. Hist. Nat. Paris, 10 (Bulletin), pp. 3–82.

David, A. (1889) Le Faune Chinoise. Bureaux des Ann. Phil. Chrét., Paris.

Davis, D. D. (1964) The Giant Panda. A morphological study of evolutionary mechanisms. Fieldiana: Zool. Mem., 3, pp. 1–339.

Demmer, H. (1958) The first giant panda since the war has reached the western world. Internat. Zoo News, 5, pp. 99–101.

Demmer, H., U. Demmer and E. Tylinek (1959) *Introducing Chi-Chi*. Spring Books. London.

De Winton, W. E. and F. W. Styan (1899) On Chinese mammals, principally from Western Szechuen. Proc. Zool. Soc. London, pp. 572–578.

Dittoe, G. (1944) Lesser pandas. Zoonooz, 17, pp. 4–5.

Edgar, J. H. (1926) Muping, the land of the giant panda. China J. Sci. and Arts, 5, pp. 183–184.

Edgar, J. H. (1929) Visiting Muping, the land of the giant panda. China J., 11, pp. 256–257.

Edgar, J. H. (1930) The haunts of the giant panda. J. West China Border Res. Soc. Chengtu, 3, p. 29.

Engelmann, C-H. (1938) Uber die Grossauger Szetschwans, Sikongs, und Ostibetts. Zs. f. Säugetierkde., 13 (Sonderheft), pp. 1–76.

Faussek, V. (1906) Biologische Untersuchungen in Transkaspien. St. Petersburg, Zap. Russ. Geogr. Obsc., 27 (2), pp. 1–192.

Fitter, R. (1963) Giant Panda. *Animals,* 1 (1), pp. 19–21.

Flower, W. H. (1869) On the value of the characters of the base of the cranium in the classification of the order Carnivora, and on the systematic position of *Bassaris* and other disputed forms. Proc. Zool. Soc. London, pp. 4–37.

Flower, W. H. (1870) On the anatomy of *Aelurus fulgens.* Fr. Cuv. Proc. Zool. Soc. London, pp. 752–769.

Flower, W. H. (1883) Article Mammalia. Ency. Brit. 9th Edition, 15, p. 441.

Flower, W. H. and R. Lydekker (1891) *Mammals Living and Extinct.* Adam and Charles Black, London.

Fox, H. M. (Editor) (1949) *Abbé David's Diary.* Harvard University Press, Cambridge, U.S.A.

Fu-Jen, C. (1956) There are many rare animals in Peking Zoo. *Zoo Life,* 11, pp. 93–94.

Geoffroy-Saint-Hilaire, M. and F. Cuvier (1824) *Histoire Naturelle des Mammiferes, avec des figures originales, coloriées, desinées d'apres des animaux vivants.* Paris, 1824–42, 2 (see p. 203).

Gervais, P. (1870) Mémoire sur les formes cérébrales propres aus carnivores vivants et fossiles. Nouv. Arch. Mus. Hist. Nat. Paris, (1) 6 (Bulletin), pp. 103–162.

Gervais, P. (1875) De l'*Ursus melanoleucus* de l'Abbé Armand David. Gervais Jour. Zool., 4, pp. 79–87.

Goss, L. J. (1940) Acute hemorrhagic gastro-enteritis in a giant panda. Zoologica, 25, pp. 261–262.

Goss, L. J. (1942) How are the giant pandas? Bull. New York Zool. Soc., 45, pp. 120–122.

Graham, D. C. (1942) How the baby pandas were captured. Bull. New York Zool. Soc., 45, pp. 19–23.

Gray, J. E. (1864) On the Ursidae. Proc. Zool. Soc. London, pp. 707–709.

Gregory, W. K. (1936) On the phylogenetic relationships of the giant panda (*Ailuropoda*) to other arctoid Carnivora. Amer. Mus. Nov. No. 878, pp. 1–29.

Haas, F. (1911) Der tibetanische Bär. Ber. Senckenberg Naturf. Ges., 42, pp. 259–261.

Haas, G. (1957) Ein Bambus-Bär im Frankfurter Zoo. Kosmos, Stuttgart, 54, pp. 405–410.

Haas, G. (1959) Ein Bambus-Bär zu Gast. Umschau, 59, pp. 198–199.

Haas, G. (1963) Beitrag zum verhalten des Bambusbären (*Ailuropus melanoleucus*). Zool. Gart. Leipzig, 27, pp. 225–233.

Hardwicke, T. (1827) Description of a new Genus of the Class

Mammalia, from the Himalaya Chain of Hills between Nepaul and the snowy mountains. Read 6th November 1821. Trans. Linn. Soc., 15 (7), pp. 161–165.

Harkness, R. (1938) *The Lady and the Panda*. Nicholson and Watson, London.

Harkness, R. (1938) *The Baby Giant Panda*. Carrick and Evans, New York.

Heck, H. (1939) Der Bambusbär oder Riesenpanda. Sonderheft der Munchner Tierpark-Zeitschrift: Das Tier und Wir.

Heck, L. and H. Weigold (1939) Ein lebender Bambusbär in Deutschland; in einem Flugblatt über die "Sonderschau Bambusbär oder Riesen-Panda des Berliner Zoologischen Gartens.

Heuvelmans, B. (1958) *On the Track of Unknown Animals*. Rupert Hart-Davies, London.

Hill, C. (1946) The story of Lien-Ho. *Zoo Life*, 1, pp. 72–75.

Hill, W. C. O. (1951) Report of the Society's Prosector for the year 1950. (Death of Lien-Ho.) Proc. Zool. Soc. London, 121, p. 649.

Hodgson, B. H. (1847) On the cat-toed Subplantigrades of the sub-Himalayas. J. Asiatic Soc. Bengal, 16, pp. 1113–1129.

Hunter, W. W. (1896) *Life of Brian Houghton Hodgson*. John Murray, London.

Hutchins, M. (1964) *The Book of the Teddy Bear*. Mills and Boon, London.

Jacobi, A. (1923) Zoologische Ergebnisse der Walter Stötznerschen Expedition nach Scetschwan, Osttibet und Tschili auf Grund der Sammlingen Dr. Hugo Weigolds. II. Mammalia. Abh. Ber. Mus. Dresden, 16 (1), pp. 1–22.

Kan, O. and T. Shu-Hua (1964) In the Peking Zoo—the first baby Giant Panda. Bull. New York Zool. Soc., 67, pp. 44–46.

Kidd, W. (1904) Note on the arrangement of the hair on the nasal region of *Aeluropus melanoleucus*. Proc. Zool. Soc. London, p. 373.

Lankester, E. R. (1901) On the affinities of *Aeluropus melanoleucus*. Trans. Linn. Soc. Lond., Zoology, 8 (6), p. 163.

Lauer, E. W. (1949) Certain olfactory centres of the forebrain of the giant panda (*Aeluropoda melanoleuca*). J. Comp. Neurol. Philadelp., 90 (2), pp. 213–241.

Leicester, C. W. (1938) We receive a Giant Panda. New York Zool. Pk. Sch. News, 3 (5), June–July.

Leone, C. A. and A. L. Wiens (1956) Comparative serology of carnivores. J. Mammal., 37, pp. 11–23.

Ley, W. (1951) Dragons in Amber, Viking Press, New York.

Loesby, R. (1938) Five Giant Pandas. Field, 172, p. 1532.

Lydekker, R. (1901) Detailed description of the skull and limb-bones (of *Ailuropoda melanoleuca*). Trans. Linn. Soc. London (2) 8, pp. 166–171.

Matthew, W. D. and W. Granger (1923) New fossil mammals from the Pliocene of Szechuan, China. Bull. Amer. Mus. Nat. Hist., 48 (17), pp. 563–598.

McClure, F. A. (1943) Bamboo as panda food. J. Mammal., 24, pp. 267–268.

McIntosh, A. (1939) A new nematode, *Ascaris schroederi* from a Giant Panda, *Ailuropoda melanoleuca*. Zoologica, 24, pp. 355–357.

Mettler, F. A. and L. J. Goss (1946) The brain of the giant panda (*Ailuropoda melanoleuca*). J. Comp. Neurol. Philadelp., 84 (1), pp. 1–9.

Milne Edwards, M. H. (1868–1874) *Recherches pour servir a L'Histoire Naturelle Des Mammifères*. Masson, Paris (see Vol I, pp. 321–338).

Milne-Edwards, A. (1869) Extrait d'une lettre de même (M. l'Abbé David) datée de la principalité Thibétaine (independante) de Moupin, le 21 mars 1869. Nouv. Arch. Mus. Hist. Nat. Paris, 5 (Bulletin), p. 13.

Milne-Edwards, A. (1870) Sur quelques Mammifères du Thibet oriental. Ann. des Sci. Nat. Series 5, 13 (10), p. 1.

Milne-Edwards, A. (1870) Note sue quelques Mammifères du Thibet oriental. Compt. Rend., 70, pp. 341–342.

Mohr, E. (1939) Der Bambusbär. Aus der Natur., 16, p. 119.

Montagu, I. (1964) More about Peking's Panda. *Animals*, 3 (17), pp. 464–466.

Morris, D. (1963) The Giant Panda. Panorama, Feb., 1963, p. 10.

Morris, D. (1963) De Grote Panda. Artis, 8 (5), pp. 166–175.

Morris, D. (1964) Der grosse Panda. Freunde des Kölner Zoo, 1, pp. 10–13.

Morrison-Scott, T. S. C. (1939) The Giant Panda. *Field*, 173, p. 283.

Oboussier, R. H. (1955) Zur Kenntnis der Hypophysis des Panda (*Ailurus fulgens* F. Cuv.). Zool. Anz., 154, pp. 1–8.

Osgood, W. H. (1932) Mammals of the Kelley-Roosevelts and Delacourt Asiatic Expeditions. Field Mus. Publ. Chicago Zool., 18, pp. 193–339.

Pen, H-S. (1943) Some notes on the giant panda. Bull. Fan. Mem. Inst. Biol. Peiping. N.S., 1 (1), pp. 64–70.

Pocock, R. I. (1921) The external characters and classification of the Procyonidae. Proc. Zool. Soc. London, pp. 389–422.

Pocock, R. I. (1928) Some external characters of the Giant

Panda (*Ailuropoda melanoleuca*). Proc. Zool. Soc. London, pp. 975–981.

Pocock, R. I. (1939) The prehensile paw of the giant panda. *Nature*, 143, p. 206, p. 381.

Pocock, R. I. (1941) *Fauna of British India, Mammalia—Vol. II.* Taylor and Francis, London.

Pocock, R. I. (1946) The Panda and the Giant Panda. *Zoo Life*, 1, pp. 67–70.

Pohle, H. (1934) Karies beim Bambusbären (*Ailuropus*). Zs. f. Säugetierkde., 9, pp. 436–437.

Portevin, G. (1937) Le grand panda. Le Terre et la Vie, 7, p. 93–94.

Raven, H. C. (1936) Notes on the anatomy and viscera of the Giant Panda (*Ailuropoda melanoleuca*). Amer. Mus. Nov. No. 877, p. 1–23.

Roosevelt, K. (1930) The search for the giant panda. J. Amer. Mus. Nat. Hist., 30, pp. 3–16.

Roosevelt, K. (1933) *Hunting Trails on Three Continents* (see Chapter 3, pp. 60–91). New York.

Roosevelt, T. and K. (1929) *Trailing the Giant Panda.* Scribner's, New York.

Sage, D. (1935) Hunting the giant panda. China J., 22 (1), pp. 35–40.

Sage, D. (1935) In quest of the giant panda. J. Amer. Mus. Nat. Hist., 35, pp. 309–320.

Sage, D. (1935) In the land of the giant panda. *Field*, 166, pp. 138–139.

Sage, D. (1938) How "Pandora" came to the Zoological Park. Bull. New York Zool. Soc., 41, pp. 115–118.

Schafer, E. (1938) Der Bambusbär (*Ailuropoda melanoleuca*). Zool. Garten, Leipzig, 10, pp. 21–31.

Schneider, K. M. (1939) Einiges vom Grossen und Kleinen Panda. I. Vom Grossen Panda. Zool. Garten, Leipzig, 11, pp. 203–232.

Schneider, K. M. (1952) Vom Bambusbären. Natur. u. Volk, 82, pp. 275–283.

Sheldon, W. G. (1937) Notes on the giant panda. J. Mammal., 18, pp. 13–19.

Sicher, H. (1944) Masticatory apparatus in the giant panda and the bears. Field Mus. Pub. Chicago Zool. Ser., 29 (4), pp. 61–73.

Simpson, K. (1869) Note on *Ailurus fulgens*. Proc. Zool. Soc. London, p. 507.

Simpson, G. G. (1945) The principles of classification and a classification of mammals. Bull. Amer. Mus. Nat. Hist., 85, pp. 1–350.

Sowerby, A. de C. (1924) Giant panda and wild dogs on the Tibetan border. China J. Sci. and Arts, 2, pp. 270–271.

Sowerby, A. de C. (1932) The pandas or cat bears. China J., 17 (6), pp. 296–299.

Sowerby, A. de C. (1933) The pandas or cat bears and the true bears. China J., 19 (5), pp. 257–259.

Sowerby, A. de C. (1934) Hunting the giant panda. China J., 21 (1), pp. 30–32.

Sowerby, A. de C. (1936) *China's Natural History: A Guide to the Shanghai Museum.* Royal Asiatic Society, Shanghai.

Sowerby, A. de C. (1936) A baby panda comes to town. China J., 25 (6), pp. 335–339.

Sowerby, A. de C. (1937) The giant panda's diet. China J., 26, pp. 209–210.

Sowerby, A. de C. (1938) The lure of the giant panda. China J., 28 (5), pp. 251–254.

Sterndale, R. A. (1884) *Natural History of the Mammalia of India and Ceylon.* Thacker, Spink and Co., Calcutta.

Street, P. (1961) *Vanishing Animals; Preserving Nature's Rarities.* Faber and Faber, London.

Swinton, W. E. (1946) The Giant Panda. *Ill. London News*, 208, p. 662.

Tee-Van, J. (1942) Two pandas—China's gift to America. Bull. New York Zool. Soc., 45, pp. 3–18.

Thomas, O. (1902) On the panda of Sze-chuen. Ann. Mag. Nat. Hist., 10, pp. 251–252.

Trouessart, E. L. (1885) Catalogue des Mammifères vivant et fossiles. Fascicule IV. Carnivores. Extr. de Bull. Soc. d'Etudes sci. d'Angers, 15, pp. 1–108.

Vevers, G. (1946) Lien-Ho, the Giant Panda. Script of B.B.C. broadcast, 20th May 1946.

Wall, F. (1908) Birth of Himalayan cat-bears (*Aelurus fulgens*) in captivity. J. Bombay Nat. Hist. Soc., 18, pp. 903–904.

Waring, R. A. and R. Harkness (1937) *Su-Lin. The Real Story of a Baby Giant Panda.* Rand McNally and Co., Chicago.

Weigold, H. (1924) Weitere Bemerkungen Dr. Weigolds zu den gesammelten Säugetieren in Zool. Ergeb. Walter. Stötzners' Exped. Szetschwan. Abh. Ber. Mus. Dresden, 16 (2), pp. 71–76.

Weitzel, K. (1949) Neue Wirbeltiere aus dem Mitteleozän von Mersel bei Darmstadt. Abh. Senckenb. naturf. Ges. 1949, No. 480, pp. 1–24.

Wendt, H. (1956) *Out of Noah's Ark*. Weidenfeld and Nicholson, London.

Wilson, E. H. (1913) *A Naturalist in Western China*. New York.

Wood-Jones, F. (1939) The forearm and manus of the Giant Panda, *Ailuropoda melanoleuca*, M-Edw., with an account of the mechanism of its grasp. Proc. Zool. Soc. London, B, 109, pp. 113–129.

Wood-Jones, F. (1939) The "thumb" of the giant panda. *Nature*, 143, p. 157, p. 246.

Woodward, A. S. (1915) On the skull of an extinct mammal related to *Aeluropus* from a cave in the ruby mines at Mogok, Burma, Proc. Zool. Soc. London, pp. 425–428.

Yee, C. (1939) *Chin-Pao* and the Giant Pandas. *Country Life*, London.

Yee, C. (1941) *The Story of Ming*. Puffin Books, London.

Yee, C. (1941) *Chin-Pao at the Zoo*. Methuen, London.

Young, C. C. and P. T. Liu (1951) On the mammalian fauna at Koloshan. Bull. Geol. Soc. China, 30, pp. 43–90.

Zuckerman, S. (1953) The breeding seasons of mammals in captivity. Proc. Zool. Soc. London, 122, pp. 827–950.

index

Aelureidopus 205
Aeluropus 205
Aelurus 44
Ailurope 39
Ailuropoda 38, 40, 41, 182, 184, 204
Ailuropus 38, 40, 42 to 44
Ailurus 10, 11, 13, 38, 42, 147
alimentary system 155, 156, 187
Alliborne, K. 134, 136
American Museum 54, 56, 60
An'–An' 124, 137, 138, 144, 208 to 211
ancient history 22 to 24
Anderson, J. 15, 16

Baby 102
bamboo 151 to 154, 212
bamboo bear 40
Bardenfleth 183, 184
Bartlett, A. D. 16 to 19
bathing 174, 175
B.E.A. 210
Bean, E. 81, 83
Bean, R. 81
bear 23 to 25, 27 to 31, 34, 36 to 42, 44, 50, 75, 124, 148, 152, 162, 165, 168, 177, 182 to 188, 190 to 192, 197, 200
Beddard 183, 184
bei-shung 23, 25, 28, 30, 33, 36, 54
Berezovski 43, 147
Berlin Museum 48
Berlin Zoo 103
Benson, S. H. 75
bi-pedalism 176, 177
Bousfield, H. T. W. 121
brain 182, 183
breeding season 162 to 165
Brocklehurst, H. C. 60, 206
Bronx Zoo 62, 89, 91, 97
Brooke, J. W. 47
Brookfield Zoo, Chicago 83 to 88

cacomistle 183, 191, 192
calls 189, 190, 210
camouflage 179
Carter, D. T. 55 to 57, 177
cat-bear 20
Chiang Kai-Shek, Madame 92, 94, 207
Chicago Zoo 81, 83 to 88
Chi-Chi 124 to 139, 141, 144, 151, 153, 158, 160, 161, 163 to 174, 176, 178, 188, 208 to 211.
chitwa 11
chromosomes 191
civets 191
classification 181 to 192
cleaning 175
climbing 177
coati 191
cocktail 194
Colbert 183, 184, 191, 192
Cologne Zoo 103
coloration 179 to 181
conservation 130, 131, 196, 202, 204
Crandall, L. 91
crepuscular rhythm 175
Cunningham, E. 89
Cuon 177
Cutting, S. 49
Cuvier, F. 10, 11, 13, 15, 42, 205
Cynodictis 191, 192

David, Père 20, 22, 31 to 42, 46, 47, 151, 183, 203, 205
Davidson, W. 191
Davis, D. 151, 166, 169, 170, 176, 184, 186 to 188, 208
delayed implantation 165
Demmer, H. 124 to 129, 196, 197, 208, 211
Diana 84, 85, 88, 206
Dickinson, F. 90
diet 151, 157, 158, 159, 212
Disney 199
Dobson, J. 41, 42

Dolan, B. 53, 54, 82
dolls 194
Dopey 102, 206
Dresden 48
Du Vaucel, A. 11 to 13

Edgar, J. H. 22, 47
Ellerman 183, 184
emblems 196
evolution of pandas 181 to 192

facial expression 173
feeding 17 to 19, 46, 47, 150 to 155, 158, 159, 212
feet 152, 153, 185
fiery fox 12
fire-coloured cat 10
Flower, W. H. 20, 183, 184
folklore 22, 27
fox 20
Fox, H. 41
Frankfurt Zoo 103, 126
Fry, D. B. 189, 190

geographical distribution 146 to 149
Gervais 183, 184
gestation 165, 209
Goodwin, G. 179
Goss 183, 184
Graham, D. C. 25, 54, 92 to 94
Granada TV 128
Grandma 102, 109, 167, 169, 206, 211
Granger, W. 205
Gregory 183 to 185
growth rate 159 to 162
Grumpy 102, 206
guts 155, 156, 187

habitat 149, 150
Hangchow 209
Hannover Zoo 103

Happy 97, 98, 102 to 104, 126, 171, 206, 207, 211
Harbin 208, 209
Hardwicke, T. 11, 13, 205
Harkness, R. 23, 63 to 69, 71 to 78, 80 to 85, 90, 100, 101, 203, 206, 211
Harkness, W. 62 to 64, 67, 74, 89
harlequin bear 40
Heuvelmans, B. 23
Hindle, E. 116
Hodgson, B. H. 12 to 14, 19
ho-shien 28
Hsing-Hsing 124, 208
hsiung-maou 28
hua-hsiung 28
Hyenarctos 40, 183

intestines 155, 156, 187

Japan 23 to 25
Jardin des Plantes 13, 42
Jarvis, C. 209
jaws 154

Kan, O. 141
Kelley, W. V. 49
kinkajou 191
Korea 209
Kunming Zoo 208

Lamour, D. 88
Lankester, R. E. 42 to 44, 183, 184
Lao Tsang 68, 69
Leipzig Zoo 103, 171
Leone 184, 190
leopard 177, 178
Ley, W. 23, 74
Li 36, 37
Lien-Ho 117 to 124, 128, 166, 207, 211
Li-Li 141, 143, 159, 161, 162, 208, 209
Lin-Lin 159, 161, 162, 208, 209
locomotion 175 to 177
Lolos 50 to 52
London Zoo 16, 17, 52, 75, 102, 104, 109, 110, 113, 116, 117, 119, 123, 124, 126, 128, 130, 137, 138, 143, 153, 158, 163, 188, 207 to 209
longevity 164, 165, 211
lordosis 167
Los Angeles Zoo 138
Lydekker, R. 44, 183, 184

Madden, C. 134, 136
Marshall Field Expedition 53, 62
masturbation 174
Matthew, W. D. 205
McClure, F. A. 212
Mei-Lan 87, 88, 90, 96, 98, 124, 165, 166, 169, 178, 207, 211
Mei-Mei 88, 96, 166, 206, 207, 211
Mettler 183, 184
miacids 191
Milne-Edwards, A. 37 to 40, 42, 44, 183, 184, 205
Ming 104 to 110, 113, 114, 120, 128, 162, 206, 207, 211
Ming-Ming 141, 143, 159, 161, 162, 208, 209
Mivart 183, 184
Montagu, I. 141, 143, 169, 208
Morrison-Scott 183, 184
Morton, S. 136, 163 to 165, 188
Moscow Zoo 124, 137, 138, 208, 209
Munich Zoo 103
musculature 187

Nanking Museum 65, 72
Nanking Zoo 208, 209
Nurnberg Zoo 103

Oeming, A. 143
olingo 191

Pan 91, 92, 207, 211
Pan-dah 91, 92, 95, 97, 98, 162, 166, 207, 211, 212
Pandarctos 183
Pan-dee 91, 92, 95, 97, 162, 166, 207, 211, 212
Pandora 90 to 92, 162, 206, 207, 211
Pao-Pei 97, 98, 162, 166, 207, 211
Paris 37, 41, 42, 103
pei-shung 23, 38
Peking Zoo 124, 125, 130, 139 to 144, 161, 170, 177, 196, 197, 208, 209
pelt 23, 25, 30
Pen, Hung-Shou 147, 150, 151, 179
penis 187, 188
Pereira, G. E. 47

Philadelphia 53
Phlaocyon 192
Ping-Ping 124, 208, 210, 211
Pi-Pi 141, 208, 209
Pocock, R. 52, 167 to 169, 183
polar bear 24, 25, 30
Polo, Marco 24
popularity 197 to 204
Potanin 43
predators 157, 177 to 181
Procyon 44
Pyongyang 209

raccoon 12, 20, 38, 182 to 185, 188, 190 to 192
radial sesamoid 153
Raven 183, 184
red fox 20
red panda 10 to 20, 42, 146, 176, 181 to 185, 188, 192, 205
relationships 181 to 192
respiration 187
Roosevelts 48 to 54, 60, 82, 205

Sage, A. 55, 56, 82, 91
Sage, D. 55, 57, 58, 60, 82, 89, 175, 206
St. Louis Zoo 97, 103, 207
scent-marking 168, 170 to 174, 188, 210
Schaefer, E. 53, 54, 60, 151, 206
scratching 175
Segall 183, 184
Selenarctos 177
serology 184, 190, 191
sexual behaviour 163 to 165
sex differences 166 to 171
sex organs 166 to 171, 187, 188, 201, 210
Shanghai Zoo 208, 209
Sheldon, W. 55, 57, 60, 151, 156, 175, 176, 178, 179, 206
Shu-Hua 141
Simpson, G. 183, 184
Simpson, H. 15, 16
sixth claw 40, 152, 153, 185, 199
skeleton 185, 186
skull 184, 184
skunk 179, 180
sleeping behaviour 175
sleeping mats 25, 26
Smith, M. 106, 107

Smith, Tangier 53, 54, 62, 64, 67, 73 to 78, 100 to 102, 109, 203, 206, 211
Sosnovsky, I. 209, 210
Sowerby, A. de C. 23, 75, 147
spear-trap 29, 30
Spooner, R. C. 90, 206, 211
Ssu-Mao 124
Steele, A. T. 85, 86, 98, 211
Stoetzner Expedition 47, 48
Styan, F. W. 43
Styan's panda 147
Su-Lin 72 to 77, 80 to 85, 89, 90, 92, 162, 166, 167, 169, 194, 206, 211
Sung 104, 106, 107, 109, 110, 166, 167, 169, 206, 207, 211
swimming 175

Tang 104, 105, 107, 108, 110, 167, 169, 206, 207, 211
taxonomy 181 to 192
teddy bear 194, 202, 203

teeth 154, 183 to 185
Tee-Van, J. 93, 95, 96, 207, 211, 212
Teh, Ma 117 to 119, 211
territory 172 to 174
tooth development 162

Union 117, 207
Unity 117, 207
Ursus 37, 38, 44, 176, 177, 182, 205
U.S. National Museum 54

Vevers, G. 102
Vincennes Zoo 103, 207
viscera 183
vocalizations 189, 210

Wallich, N. 11
Wang 67, 76
Wassuland 46
Weber 40, 183, 184
weights 164 to 166, 210, 211

Weigold, H. 47, 48, 75, 177, 205
Wei-han, Den 91 to 93, 211
Wendt, H. 23, 74
West China Union University 25, 54, 89 to 91
Wha 11, 13
Whipsnade 108 to 110, 207
white bear 23 to 25, 34, 36, 37, 41
Wiens 184, 190
wild dog 177
Wilson, E. H. 46, 47
Winge 183, 184
Woodward 205
World Wildlife Fund 196, 197

Yeh, G. K. C. 116
Young, J. 49, 53, 54, 65
Young, Q. 65, 67 to 72, 76

Zappey, W. 46
Zoology Jones 64 to 66